CHINA'S WARLORDS

China's Warlords

David Bonavia

HONG KONG
OXFORD UNIVERSITY PRESS
OXFORD NEW YORK
1995

Oxford University Press

Oxford   New York
Athens   Auckland   Bangkok   Bombay
Calcutta   Cape Town   Dar es Salaam   Delhi
Florence   Hong Kong   Istanbul   Karachi
Kuala Lumpur   Madras   Madrid   Melbourne
Mexico City   Nairobi   Paris   Singapore
Taipei   Tokyo   Toronto

and associated companies in
Berlin   Ibadan

Oxford is a trade mark of Oxford University Press

First published 1995

Published in the United States
by Oxford University Press, New York

© Oxford University Press 1995

British Library Cataloguing in Publication Data
available

Library of Congress Cataloging-in-Publication Data
Bonavia, David, 1940–
China's warlords/David Bonavia.
p. cm.—(Oxford in Asia paperbacks)
Includes bibliographical references and index.
ISBN 0-19-586179-5
1. China—History—Warlord period, 1916–1928. 2. China—Politics
and government—1912–1949. 3. Generals—China. I. Title.
II. Series.
DS777.36B66   1995
951.04'1—dc20   95-3206
CIP

Printed in Hong Kong
Published by Oxford University Press (China) Ltd
18/F Warwick House, Taikoo Place, 979 King's Road, Quarry Bay, Hong Kong

Editor's Note

DAVID BONAVIA, my husband, completed this book in the early 1980s. The book remained unpublished at the time of his untimely death in September 1988, at the age of 48.

In 1992, our friend and renowned scholar of the Republican warlord period, Dr Diana Lary of the University of British Columbia, Vancouver, Canada, visited Hong Kong and asked to read the manuscript. Encouraged by her enthusiasm, by the new contribution she thought it made to the understanding of this confusing and complex period of China's twentieth-century history, and by its relevance to the current situation with regard to regionalism as a political characteristic, once again strongly evident in China, I approached Oxford University Press.

I sincerely thank Dr Lary for her encouragement and support. She has brought her own academic intensity to bear on aspects of the editing. Where elaboration appeared desirable, this has been included in square brackets.

To bring the text in line with current practice in the field, names of places and people figuring in the text have been put into the *pinyin* system of romanization. The few exceptions include the cities, Peking, Canton, Tientsin, Nanking and Yenan, the Yangtze river, and the political party, Kuomintang.

The book, otherwise, is entirely David's work — his final contribution to Chinese studies.

JUDY BONAVIA
HONG KONG
OCTOBER 1993

Foreword

THIS BOOK was written in the early 1980s, and was unfinished at the time of David Bonavia's death. It was written at a time when Chinese warlords had slipped into scholarly oblivion. In China the study of warlords had been taboo in the 1950s and early 1960s, since all that could be said about them at times of Marxist orthodoxy was that they were 'feudal relics' and 'running dogs of imperialism'. During the Cultural Revolution, no academic work was done at all. In the West there was a spurt of research and writing on warlords in the 1960s and 1970s; after that the subject seemed to die, perhaps exhausted by the amount of work done in a fairly short period (see Bibliography).

Over the past few years interest in warlordism has re-emerged. In China a surge of activity has seen the start of new research, and the republication of memoirs and biographies of warlords written in the 1930s and 1940s. This work is part of a complete re-evaluation of the Republican period. In the gloomy context of modern Chinese history as now revealed, which includes the horrors of the Japanese occupation, the Civil War, and the Cultural Revolution, the warlords look less horrible than they did at the time. Some warlords have emerged as something close to national heroes. Feng Yuxiang has had a big revival, largely because of his reputation for honesty and directness, and was referred to recently in the *People's Daily* as a 'patriotic general'.[1] Zhang Xueliang's recent release from prison in Taiwan, after more then fifty years of incarceration, has revived interest in him and his father Zhang Zuolin. The recent revival and growth of regional loyalties in China as the retreat from ideology

---

[1] *Renmin ribao*, 21 February 1993, p. 5.

gains strength has led many regions to focus on their local heroes — often warlords. Yan Xishan has re-entered the hall of heroes in Shanxi; Lu Rongting, Li Zongren, and Bai Chongxi are all revered in Guangxi; Long Yun is the darling of Yunnan. Only the truly awful warlords have been denied local hero status — for example, Zhang Zongchang in Shandong.

There is another, sad reason for the revival of interest in Chinese warlordism: the sudden and evil flowering of warlordism in other countries. The warring factions in Somalia and the former Yugoslavia may be based on religious and ethnic tensions, but the flourishing of warlordism is also dependent on the breakdown of once unitary political and military structures, the free flow of arms and the willing recruitment of young men — the phenomena which once contributed to warlordism in China. What was once seen as a strange and exotic phenomenon is now something the world watches on television every night. The study of warlords now has a contemporary relevance.

No book on warlordism is easy to read; there is such an overload of events that there is a constant confusion of dates and activities, of cities being captured, lost, and recaptured, and individual warlords rising, falling, and rising again. The confusions can make one's head spin, but this should not detract from the anguish and fear involved for those caught up in warlord wars. The insecurity and suffering of the Chinese people in the 1920s and 1930s were not as public as those of the Somalis and Bosnians today, but they were real, and have left their influence on contemporary China. They may pale by contrast with the Japanese invasion or the Cultural Revolution, but the divisiveness they engendered paved the way for those tragedies.

DIANA LARY
VANCOUVER
SEPTEMBER 1993

Preface

THE WARLORD PERIOD — from 1912 until roughly the beginning of the Second World War — is one of the most extraordinary and colourful in the whole of Chinese history. It is
also highly complex, and a full historical treatment would
require many volumes. So most English-language studies of
the period until now have focused either on individual warlords, or on the history of the provinces they ruled, or on
warlords as a socio-political phenomenon. The purpose of
this book is to describe the careers and characters of a number of warlords in a readable form, and to attempt to locate
them in history as regards their politics, methods, military
prowess, life-style, ethics, and ideals. Frequent reference has
been made to the economic and social conditions which
accompanied warlordism in China, but this is primarily a
book about a group of historical figures rather than an essay
in social history. I hope it will be of interest to some sinolo-
gists as well as general readers and students of the period, for
whom a handy outline is badly needed.

A complex task is the attribution of ranks to the warlords.
The rank of marshal (*yuanshuai*) and that of general (*jiang-
jun*) are particularly difficult to allocate, since the more powerful warlords conveyed titles on themselves, and the government in Peking pasted them on political favourites, at
moments in time often hard to ascertain. I have pursued the
system of calling a warlord 'general' if he controlled only one
province, and 'marshal' if he controlled two or more. This
may seem somewhat arbitrary, but it does convey a rough
conception of the subjects' respective strength and power,
which mattered much more than ranks.

I am grateful for all the hard work my wife Judy has put
into the research and production of this book, and to

Professor Jerome Ch'en for helpful suggestions and correc-
tions regarding the chapter on Zhang Zuolin.

DAVID BONAVIA

Contents

Plates

(between pages 94 and 95)

1. Sun Yatsen, the 'father of the Chinese Republic'.

2. Yuan Shikai (1859–1916), the 'father' of the warlord system.

3. Yuan Shikai while provisional president of the Republic of China (1912).

4. Yuan Shikai attempted to assume the title of 'emperor'. He is shown here in a ritual of homage at the Temple of Heaven.

5. General Cai E (1859–1916), the *dujun* of Yunnan, and first provincial leader openly to declare independence in opposition to the presidency of Yuan Shikai.

6. Li Yuanhong, upon his inauguration as president of the Republic in June 1916.

7. The Peking warlord, Duan Qirui, who became premier of the Republic in 1916.

8. Zhang Xun (1854–1923), the 'Pigtailed General', was governor of Anhui. He led a briefly successful move in 1917 to restore the last Qing dynasty emperor, Pu Yi, to the throne.

9. Feng Guochang (1859–1919), the governor of Jiangsu, was a major figure within the Zhili Group of warlords. He suceeded Li Yuanhong as president in 1917.

10. The Guangxi warlord, Lu Rongting.

11. Marshal Cao Kun (1862–1938), a Zhili warlord, bribed members of the parliament to elect him as president of the Republic in 1923.

12. Soldiers of the Northern Army pose with their rifles.

Chronology

1894		Sun Yatsen establishes the Xingzhonghui
1894–5		Sino-Japanese War
1898		Hundred Days Reform
1900		Boxer Rebellion
1904–5		Russo–Japanese War
1905	September	Cancellation of the imperial civil service examination system
1908	November	Death of Guangxu Emperor and Empress Dowager Cixi
1911	October	Wuchang uprising (1911 Revolution)
	December	Regent abdicates on behalf of Qing emperor. Sun Yatsen elected first president of Republic of China
1912	January	Republic proclaimed
	February	Sun resigns, Yuan Shikai becomes second president
1913	July	Second revolution (fails)
1914	August	China declares neutrality in First World War
	September	Japan occupies German holdings in Shandong
1915	January	Japan presents the twenty-one demands to China
	October	Yuan Shikai announces imperial aspirations

1916 January   Start of anti-Yuan National Protection
                  (huguo) movement
     June   Yuan dies. Li Yuanhong becomes
                  president. Duan Qirui becomes premier.

1917 June   Attempted imperial restoration
     August   China declares war on Germany
     September   Sun Yatsen sets up government in
                  Canton
     November   Duan Qirui resigns as premier

1918 January   Start of the Constitution
                  Protection (hufa) movement
     March   Duan Qirui resumes office
                  Start of Northerners' attack into Hunan
     October   Xu Shichang becomes president
     November   End of First World War

1919 May   May Fourth movement
     July   Kharakhan Declaration

1920 Summer   Anfu–Zhili war
     July   Resignation of Duan Qirui

1922   Zhili–Fengtian war
     February   Sun Yatsen launches Northern
                  Expedition (aborted)
     June   Li Yuanhong resumes presidency

1923 January   Manifesto of Kuomintang Sun–Joffe
                  Agreement
     October   Soviet advisers arrive in Canton Cao
                  Kun becomes president

1924   Second Zhili–Fengtian war

1925 March   Death of Sun Yatsen
     June   Start of the Hong Kong strike
     July   National government of Kuomintang,
                  Canton
     November   Guo Songlin revolt, Manchuria

	December	Sun Chuanfang declares autonomy from Peking
1926	April	Feng Yuxiang besieged at Nankou
	June	Start of the Northern Expedition
	September	Northern Expedition takes Wuhan
	November	Northern Expedition takes Nanchang
1927	March	Northern Expedition takes Nanking and Shanghai
	April	Kuomintang turns against Communists
	June	Feng Yuxiang, Yan Xishan go over to the Kuomintang
	December	Communist rising in Canton
1928	May	Japanese troops attack Jinan (Shandong)
	June	Assassination of Zhang Zuolin
		Kuomintang troops take Peking
1929	March	Guangxi warlords driven out of central China
	May	Feng Yuxiang rebels against Nanking government
1930	August	Nanking troops defeat Feng and Yan
1931	August	Yangtze flood
	September	Japanese occupation of Manchuria
1932	January	Japanese troops attack Shanghai (defeated)
	March	Puppet state of Manzhouguo set up
1933	February	Japanese take over Rihe
	September	Zhang Zongchang assassinated
1934	January	Fujian rebellion
	May	Zhang Jingyao assassinated
	October	Start of the Long March
1935	January	Mao Zedong becomes chairman of the Chinese Communist Party

Introduction

The Warlord Style

THE DECLINE of major ruling dynasties in China since at least as long ago as 1000 BC was usually marked by armed uprisings — whether spontaneous, in the form of peasant revolts, or planned, as in the case of military commanders who sought the throne for themselves. Armed rebellion and civil war occurred at all levels — from village clan feuds up to the power-rivalry of the leaders of whole provinces and vice-royalties, as big as fair-sized European countries of the modern age.

The Qing dynasty, which had ruled since the Manchus conquered China in 1644, proved no exception. From the 1840s on, it had been riven by wars and invasions, territorial concessions to other countries, and a major rebellion —- the Taiping movement — which nearly toppled the dynasty in the 1860s.

When the Empress Dowager Cixi died in 1908 — mysteriously on the same day as her son, the reigning emperor — power fell into the hands of an experienced military commander, Yuan Shikai, and a republic was proclaimed. Armed uprisings in different parts of the country took place in 1911 which led in October to full-scale revolution known as the Xinhai or 1911 Revolution. The exiled Dr Sun Yatsen, the 'father of the Chinese Republic', who had organized the main anti-Manchu movement from abroad, returned to China and briefly became the first president of the Republic in early 1912. He soon surrendered the position to the military strong man of China, Yuan Shikai.

The collapse of the Manchu dynasty was caused above all by the incursions of the European seafaring and trading powers in the nineteenth century. Chinese technology and martial skills were no match for the frigates of the British and French, and later the battleships and land armies of Japan and Germany. Russia hoped to infiltrate Manchuria. Other countries had interests of various kinds — Belgian railway loans, Christian missions set up by Americans and Europeans representing a score of denominations, mining interests, and arms dealers.

The unwarlike Dr Sun was poorly equipped to handle the process of military centrifugalism which set in after Yuan Shikai's death in 1916. Yuan, who had been made president of the new Republic by the Provisional Parliament, had attempted to have himself enthroned as emperor. The country split up into half a dozen main areas dominated by regional commanders, with hundreds of petty commanders and mere bandits holding out in individual cities or remote areas. These men, the most powerful of whom were called warlords in English, *dujun* or *junfa* in Chinese, were mostly professional soldiers, some trained in modern war colleges with European and Japanese advisers, or bandits who had collected enough followers to wield sufficient military force.

With the formal collapse of the dynasty and the failure of Yuan Shikai to make himself emperor, China entered into the warlord period. Though generally thought to have lasted from 1916 to 1928, in fact it continued, in a residual way, until 1937 and the Japanese invasion. Local and regional commanders gathered their troops around themselves in a system of commander–soldier relationships, which was of considerable strength in that it provided a substitute for the emperor–citizen relationship — the ideological basis of the late empire. The warlords' troops fought — when they did fight — mainly out of loyalty to their commander, and of course for food and loot. Most were mere boys. They were deficient in training, discipline, uniforms, arms, and medical supplies. Their preferred manner of fighting was to shuffle in the general direction of the enemy, loose off a shot or two without aiming, then sit down to await further orders. But they were also capable of ferocity and valour.

Modern warlordism was a specific product of the twentieth century, but its roots lie far back in Chinese history. Until the end of the third century BC, China was split into a number of kingdoms, the Warring States, and fiefdoms which expanded to absorb or conquer their neighbours, or suffered eclipse while their ruling families were massacred by victorious enemies.

Even after the unification of China under the first Qin emperor in 221 BC, military revolt and full-scale civil war were only held temporarily in abeyance. The collapse of the Qin dynasty in 210 BC was followed by a fierce war of succession in which the victorious commander, Liu Bang, founded the stable and prosperous Han dynasty. Sometimes starving or oppressed peasants formed themselves into bands with special insignia in their dress — such as the Yellow Turbans in the second century AD. Peasant rebels up until the twentieth century often practised religious or pseudo-religious cults to increase their cohesion and ensure their own victory.

The vast extent of the empire at the height of the Tang dynasty (AD 618–907) led to the creation of military governorships in outlying areas, which gradually won more and more autonomy from the central government — to the point where they could assert their military independence and even threaten the ruling dynasty.

In Chinese historical tradition, war was considered a matter of stratagems, and bluffs, more than a question of slogging it out on the battlefield. The greatest military philosopher of ancient times, Sun Tzu, had declared that 'all war is deception'. Night manoeuvres, surprise attack, treachery, bribery, and shifting alliances — the Chinese commander was admired most if he mastered all these practices and used them to the full before committing his troops to the field of battle. There was little clemency, however, and the losing side were routinely massacred or enslaved. The 'cunning Ulysses' of the Greek Odyssey would have found more to admire in Chinese warfare then the blunt Julius Caesar, who fought Rome's wars with iron discipline and brute strength.

China has its own code of military honour and gallantry, but this system was held in slight esteem by the Confucian scholar–administrators, who despised soldiers and cordially disliked war. By contrast with the European tradition, a young man of the gentry class would not especially consider himself gaining glory by taking up arms — but for the less scholastically inclined, it was one way to emoluments and power. Military commissions could often be purchased for cash.

Quite a few of the twentieth-century warlords came from the new-style military colleges with foreign instructors. Some, like Wu Peifu, one of the most powerful and durable warlords of central China, were scholars in their own right. One of the most famous, Feng Yuxiang, was a devout Christian; another was a utopian socialist. But all were profoundly affected by their knowledge of the historical wars and martial arts of China. They fought as though playing a chess game; indeed chess was considered in China an excellent metaphor for warfare.

Colourful and swaggering though many of the warlords were, some of them were thoughtful men who understood the crisis that had overtaken China. But their own inability to unite in the cause of patriotism brought all such ideas to naught.

They killed without compunction — their own men, if they breached discipline; the enemy's troops; often civilians, if they resisted rape or plunder. They used horrible tortures — death by minute slicing of the flesh; suspension by the neck in bamboo or wooden cages; breaking the victim's knees on a pile of chains; slicing limbs off bit-by-bit in a hay-chopping guillotine; branding on the face, and so on. Beating the thighs with bamboo poles until they were bruised and lacerated, and the bones fractured, was considered mild. The best any victim could hope for was the quick beheading at which Chinese executioners were expert. The heads were displayed on spikes, or over city walls and gates for the edification of the general public. Man's inhumanity to man was brought by the Chinese to a fine art.

It should be recalled that all this was not exclusive to China. The foreigners who laudably denounced torture came from societies where such things had been commonplace only two or three centuries before. And the refinements of the use of electricity, gas chambers, and horrifying medical experiment with live patients, were still things of the future in Europe.

Most of the Chinese warlords were, with some notable exceptions, highly self-indulgent, wallowing in gluttony, drunkenness, and opium, hoarding money and treasure, and taking as many concubines as they wanted. They dressed themselves and their retainers in finery and had fanciful uniforms while half-naked beggars crept by, starving (although this was something by no means unknown in the Europe of the day, for that matter, and normal in today's Latin America and India). They were superstitious, and frequently consulted omens and oracles.

To take a measured view of the Chinese warlords and their blood-thirstiness, one must consider the social and historical context in which they operated. Massacre of prisoners had been commonplace throughout Chinese history (it was nick-named 'blood for the drums'). But most warlords preferred to absorb defeated troops into their own armies. Torture was still routine in Chinese magistrates' courts in the early twentieth century. The Kuomintang (the KMT or Nationalist Party) often had recourse to it in the struggle with the Communists (who generally considered it inefficient as a means of extracting information or making converts).

Was there, none the less, something in the make-up of a typical warlord which predisposed him to callousness above and beyond the norm acceptable in China? Perhaps. The essential feature of so many of them was their humble origin, and that to get where they were in later life, they needed a thick streak of ruthlessness. Young men in the China of the day rarely became soliders if they had any other decent career open to them — and that was true from the top to the bottom of the ragged armies which fought their way to and fro across China for a quarter of a century and more. According to Professor Hsi-sheng Ch'i, a noted modern authority on the warlord period, among leading command-ers there were two ex-bandits, two former foot-soldiers, a cotton cloth pedlar, a cymbalist, and two scions of impover-ished families.[1]

The 'better class' of warlord typically came from the fam-ily of an impecunious intellectual who had failed to climb the ladder of success through the civil service examinations (which were anyway abolished in 1905, after two millennia of use). Without money, friends and influence, the best he could do for his son would be to give him a thorough grounding in the Chinese classics, even though the country was turning rapidly towards Western-style education as the new norm. The boy could then perhaps apply for entrance to a military school or academy. If the aspiring cadet had enough money, he could obtain military training in Japan, and quite a few did so.

After the death of Yuan Shikai, the centralized control of the armed forces of the Republic — already shaky since the 1911 Revolution — ceased to exist. Until the Northern Expedition in 1926 the authority of the Kuomintang barely extended beyond Guangdong province, leaving a central power vacuum. The country was plunged into a spiral of greater and greater fragmentation, in which the actual divi-sions within China were unclear and constantly shifting. As a convenient shorthand, commentators at the time often talked of China as divided into two amorphous groupings — the 'Northerners', based in Peking, and the 'Southerners',

[1] Ch'i Hsi-sheng, *Warlord Politics in China 1916–1928*, Stanford: Stanford University Press, 1976.

based in Canton. Northerners were seen as traditional, unprincipled, and venal, a procession of warlords who succeeded one another in Peking with apparent casualness. Southerners were different. They were revolutionaries, who wanted to change China and restore it to its rightful position in the world. They had a conspicuous, long-term leader, Sun Yatsen, an ideology of nationalism and (it was widely feared) socialism, and a party, the Kuomintang. Their major ambition was to launch a northern expedition which would reunify China and get rid of the northern warlords and the foreign imperialists.

The reality was less simple. Much of China was controlled neither by the Northerners or the Southerners, but by regional warlords. The Northerners' chief common characteristics were that they lived in the north, and that they were continuously involved in clique fighting with each other — among the Anfu, Zhili, and Fengtian cliques. The Southerners were more united, but much weaker; they had great difficulty in establishing and maintaining even a tiny base in Canton, and though Sun Yatsen tried twice to launch his Northern Expedition, he failed both times.

Sun died in 1925, one year before the actual Northern Expedition was launched. By this time the base in Canton and surrounding Guangdong province had been consolidated, in part with the help of Soviet advisers, sent to Canton as a result of an agreement between Sun Yatsen and Moscow in 1923. One of the leading figures in the emergence of the southern military was Chiang Kaishek, who himself had been to Moscow for military training. On his return in 1924 he started the training of the revolutionary army which would sweep through China in 1926 and 1927 on the Northern Expedition. Chiang was the overall commander for the expedition, but much of the front-line fighting was done by Guangdong armies not directly under his control, notably the Fourth (Iron) Army, or armies which had only recently joined the Kuomintang, such as the Seventh Army from Guangxi.

With the breakdown of even a pretence of centralized command, officers commanding forces from company or even platoon size upwards became a law unto themselves in the areas they occupied. Thus, although history mainly remembers a score or so of famous big warlords, with whole armies under their command, China was actually administered — if one could call it that — by thousands of middle-rank officers whose loyalty to their superiors at, say, the provincial level was tenuous to say the least.

The other well-trodden path to warlord status was banditry. Destitute peasants, small artisans, or unemployed soldiers roamed the countryside, living off what little plunder they could find. Since the warlord armies were often paid and fed through levies and confiscations from the civilian population, the latter had little to choose between anarchy caused by bandits or 'government' by whichever warlord was dominant in their locality. Some soldiers hovered perpetually between banditry and the service of warlords. From the warlords they usually got only small and irregular pay, but at least clothing and food were guaranteed and there was a chance in the course of military campaigns of looting in towns and cities, where the pickings were better than in the countryside. Merchants either hired armed guards to protect their goods in transit, or took the chance of paying *lijin* (tolls) to warlord troops or being robbed and perhaps murdered by bandits. Banditry was no great social stigma for those who later rose to prominence in more-or-less respectable commands.

The traditional Chinese way for a bandit to become respectable was for him to rally with his men and arms to the side of a local warlord or petty commander, perhaps helping track down and liquidate some rival band. He, with his troops, could then be incorporated in the warlord's forces with a rank roughly commensurate with his talents or the number of men he brought with him. The group usually remained intact, in case it should seem expedient at any time to break away and return to banditry.

The inherent contradictions between a life centred on war, and the doctrines of important religions or progressive political creeds, make it understandable that the great majority of the warlords — with a few outstanding exceptions — were dedicated to just three things: their personal security, pleasure, and self-aggrandisement. In warfare they changed sides according to the progress of a campaign, and if the commander did not care to go over to the enemy when the going got sticky, his men might make the decision for him by defecting.

Though most of them would have professed a vague patriotism or, more likely, loyalty to the province of their birth, the warlords were not usually anti-foreign. In his early career, the Kuomintang leader Chiang Kaishek was more xenophobic than any warlord who might be getting arms and other supplies from foreigners. It was difficult to hate foreigners when they were designing trench mortars for you — as was the case with Frank Sutton, a one-armed British officer turned arms-smuggler, who became adviser (with the rank of general) to the Manchurian warlord Zhang Zuolin. Zhang's long career as ruler of the vast lands of Manchuria owed much to his pragmatism in dealing with foreigners, in particular the Japanese. The bigger warlords also needed foreign contacts to help them salt away their fortunes in the safe and secure vaults of foreign banks in Shanghai and Tientsin, or to make lucrative investments in partnership with foreign firms.

The majority of warlords whose character has been described by contemporary writers were noted for their deep-seated opportunism. The provincial ruler in his grandiose headquarters, the regimental commander garrisoning a city, the battalion commander with a county to roam — down to the bandit who brought a dozen men into warlord service — their primary motives were security, wealth, and power. In their dealings with each other, the only fairly dependable link was direct loyalty — which the Chinese call *guanxi* — between a former teacher and pupil, former classmates at military academy, or relatives by blood or marriage. That is why the big warlords were careful to keep their subordinate commanders locked in a two-way relationship — a radial pattern, so to speak, in which contact among the spokes was restricted though not wholly ruled out.

Most warlords were ostentatious in their dress and life-style, with the notable exception of Feng Yuxiang, who wore the same plain dress as his soldiers. Contemporary photographs show warlords sporting glittering uniforms copied from the countries which had most influenced their concept of the modern commander-in-chief. Zhang Zuolin positively swathed himself in gold braid, orders and decorations, epaulettes, gleaming buckles, and white gloves. His small-peaked cap suggested that he was modelling himself on a Russian officer in the army of the tsar. Others preferred French-style *kepis*, the British First World War uniform with Sam Browne belt, or helmets with enormous plumes. (Chiang Kaishek favoured an American-style officer's uniform with its high-peaked cap.)

The rank and file, it goes without saying, were less sump-tuously attired. Usually they wore a peaked or padded cap, tunic, baggy trousers, and puttees, with cloth shoes. Shortage of winter clothing was a recurring problem, and washing facilities poor.

The central problem facing every warlord was finance. They were notorious for their exactions — for the provincial coffers were often empty when they seized power, and nei-ther the 'government' in Peking nor the Kuomintang regime in Canton was in a position to hand out big subsidies. Each warlord had to make shift for himself and his men, who were astonishingly patient as long as they were fed, though mutinies by unpaid troops did occur.

Every dodge in history was used to raise funds: custom dues at provincial boundaries, *lijin* (or tolls) along the way, taxes on every imaginable pretext. Zhang Zongchang in Shandong, one of the cruellest and most vicious of all the warlords, taxed tobacco seeds, military pensions, firewood and straw, dogs, dwellings, opium-pipe lighters, vegetables, brothels, and chickens, to name but a few heads of extortion.

The south-western warlords were the most fortunate in the matter of revenue, for they imposed a heavy transit tax on opium being moved out of the mountainous provinces of Yunnan and Guizhou en route for Canton, the main distribution centre.

J.O.P. Bland, a well-known British journalist, wrote in 1920:

> To appeal to the patriotism of the Tuchuns [dujuns] (big warlords) would be going to the goat's house for wool. It is reckoned by competent observers that every one of them (with two possible exceptions) has amassed a large fortune, and many are known to be multi-millionaires. Some of them have invested vast sums in real estate at the Treaty Ports, whilst others have deposited their wealth in foreign banks. Others, again, are looking about for safe investments in Anglo-Chinese and Sino-American companies — a fact that has a good deal to do with the development of the 'co-operative enterprise' idea. It has been estimated that, during the last eight years, the twenty-two Tuchuns, among them, and the metropolitan officials have 'squeezed' enough money to pay off four-fifths of China's national debt; a good deal of this money has been 'squeezed' from foreign loans and concession contracts ...[2]

Some provincial warlords took the path of inflation, issuing debased coinage or unbacked paper currency. Naturally it helped them not at all in the long run, because the merchants and general public were not so stupid as to accept phoney money for long.[3]

---

[2] J.O.P. Bland, *China, Japan and Korea*, London: Heinemann, 1921, p. 93.

[3] Sun Yatsen was also incredibly naïve about inflation, according to his Australian adviser, A. M. Donald, who quotes him as suggesting that China print huge amounts of paper money and thereby become the richest country in the world.

Tortuous problems of exchange rates and weights and measures bedevilled inter-provincial commerce, which sank to an all-time low in the warlord period. Some of the more progressive warlords, like Yan Xishan, launched industrialization schemes to make their provinces less vulnerable to outside economic pressures and less dependent on their neighbours for supplies of various goods. Yan was the most durable of all the warlords, ruling the province of Shanxi for over thirty years. This policy of self-sufficiency increased protectionist pressures in the individual provinces, none of which wanted to see its silver or good copper coinage being drained away to others.

The bigger warlords also strove to become self-sufficient in the simpler forms of guns, ammunition, and grenades. This was particularly necessary since there was often little standardization of weaponry, the troops having been supplied from any available source — the guns of fallen comrades, enemies, or captives, shipments from foreign merchants and governments, or issues by superior commanders.

To be based in a provincial capital or county town gave the warlord the power to use the existing civil administration — such as it was — and the traditional revenues of the area. It also put in his gift a variety of civil and military appointments which, hollow though they might be in reality, bestowed prestige and sometimes income. So a great deal of fighting was concerned with the capture or holding of significant towns and cities, and some quite long sieges were mounted. The besieged usually had the advantage, unless they ran out of food or their commander venally went over to the other side.

What of the warlords and their soldiers as fighting men? The China of the late nineteenth and early twentieth century was not devoid of stirring martial exploits. Despite the humiliations suffered at the hands of a growing number of foreign countries, remarkable battles were fought within China during the period of the Taiping Rebellion which shook the foundations of the Manchu throne in the 1850s and early 1860s. Finally suppressed with the aid of the British General C. G. Gordon, the pseudo-Christian Taipings were a redoubtable fighting force, their main weakness being the antiquated nature of their weapons and tactics.

By the end of the nineteenth century, there were still plenty of men in China who could recall the *gloire et servitudes* of the military life and pass on their experiences to their sons and grandsons. They also knew what it was like to mount a revolution against the Manchu regime, which enjoyed no exaggerated reverence among the Chinese people. Some of the spirit of the Taiping rebels was undoubtedly passed on to the makers of the 1911 Revolution and the warlord regime which sprang up after it.

Although the troops were ill-trained practically everywhere, they were not all lacking in valour. It was traditional Chinese practice to avoid battle if the serious risk of defeat was present. Soldiers and commanders might defect to the enemy if they thought their own side was facing certain defeat. But if affronted by the enemy's arrogance, or pushed into a corner, Chinese soldiers could be 'psyched up' to make a desperate resistance or a gallant charge. Then the tradition-minded among them would strip to the waist and tie turbans round their hair as a signal of their willingness to die, and rush the enemy with cutlasses and spears if there were not enough rifles to go round. (Experience in the Korean War showed that despite their reputation for prudence, Chinese soldiers could give the most modern and well-trained armies a tough fight when their morale was sufficiently engaged. The stoicism of the Chinese in the face of imminent death has been attested by numerous travellers who witnessed beheadings and other executions.)

An aspect of the warlord period which set it apart from earlier periods of civil war in China, was the relative respect which the military leaders paid to foreign consuls and missionaries. Foreigners were molested and killed from time to time, especially during the Boxer uprising of 1900, but such incidents grew fewer as the twentieth century wore on. The Boxer Rebellion was an outpouring of xenophobic rage against foreign incursion in China. It started in Shandong, directed against German missionaries and railway builders, and then spread throughout north China, and especially to Peking. The warlords were aware that harming foreigners might bring down the retribution of their government, through gunboat attacks, boycott, aid to the warlord's enemies, or denial of sanctuary to him in, say, Tientsin or Shanghai, if he were ever overthrown and in flight. Some of the consuls were men of great erudition and courage who were familiar with the Chinese language and many of its dialects, and some warlords took to asking them to mediate in their disputes and even battles. Meyrick Hewlett, a British consul, gives a highly-coloured account of his intervention in just such a situation when the troops of Yunnan and Guizhou were fighting in Sichuan. Of course, like most Chinese who had never travelled abroad, the typical warlord thought any foreigner a pretty weird bird but given the choice of a friendly or hostile relationship he would usually opt for the former, if only to the extent of correctness.

The Japanese, in particular, were intrigued with some warlords in north China, where they were preparing the excision of Manchuria. They expected obedience; when Zhang Zuolin made an alliance with the Kuomintang in early 1928, they assassinated him. Other foreign powers were less attracted by alliances with individual warlords: it went against the European tradition of relations among nations, which was by no means altruistic, but which tended to see international conflict in terms of nation-against-nation, not subversion of the other fellow's troops.

Western governments were wary of their subjects becoming involved in illicit arms deals with Chinese warlords: their own machinations in carving up her wealth were complex enough, without adventurers blundering in. Businessmen and concession-hunters, of course, had to have some sort of relations with the local satraps, but usually took the easy course of bribing them into benignity.

This was easy enough, for nearly all the warlords were fascinated by the skills, luxuries, and trappings of the modern, that is, Western world. Huge limousines, armoured cars, aeroplanes, automatic pistols, gramophones, pianos, cameras, wireless sets, Homburg hats, bathrooms with hot and cold running water, gold watches, fountain pens, binoculars, brandy — all these and others represented the proverbial candy-shop for the successful warlord. Some also developed a taste for European women, especially White Russian refugees. For those based in or near cities with big foreign communities, there was horse-racing, and there were casinos. The cinema was in its infancy, and jazz bands and crooners crowded Shanghai's nightclubs: whether their music was to the taste of the Chinese or not, its novelty guaranteed its success.

Nor were warlords averse to the more traditional pleasures of Chinese society, if they were among the minority with a good education. They enjoyed huge banquets with the most exotic ingredients, 'sing-song girls', concubines, classical books, calligraphy and painting, poetry, music performed on the Chinese flute, zither, and lute, Chinese opera, moonlight boat parties, picnics, rare brands of tea, tonics and cordials, *objets d'art*, curios, and antiques.

In their political role, the warlords above all were realists. They eschewed sentimentality in their relations with others of their type, except in the case of the most intimate and long-standing cases of *guanxi*. If one warlord received an invitation to dine with another, it was uncertain whether he would get agreeably drunk or be assassinated. (Murdering one's foe at a banquet is one of the most hallowed traditions in Chinese politics.) What they dreaded most was to lose their base area — however large or small — and become itinerant mercenaries allied with whomever would give them a place to bivouac and make exactions on the countryside. In their base area they were at least familiar with the dialects and customs of the local people, with whom their relations, however, were more likely to be edgy than friendly. (Only

Feng Yuxiang, the Christian general, used to be welcomed in strange provinces and was actually begged to stay!)

Regionalism was very strong, and a warlord was better accepted if he had been born in the province or county which he made his base. Chinese provincials would usually prefer a tyrant whom they knew and understood than a warlord from the next province, with which they had probably been at daggers-drawn for centuries. There might be kinship and — strongest of all — marriage ties. And the soldiery could be expected to fight more readily for a local man than for a stranger.

J.O.P. Bland noted the role played by antipathies between northern and southern Chinese in the civil wars. He quotes a young intellectual as writing: 'For military operations against the North, the South depends on Governors (warlords) who are just as selfish as their northern colleagues. It also receives, as its allies, brigands or military leaders who have some personal grievance against the North and who desire to gratify their greed and ambition by taking advantage of the great quarrel between the constitutionalists and the militarists.'[4] (During the Northern Expedition, Chiang Kaishek's armies were swollen by defections from provinces south of the Yangtze; defections by Northern units to the Southern armies were almost unheard of.) As William W. Whitson puts it:

> Only a judicious concern for the realities of his military power *vis-à-vis* that of his adversaries governed a warlord's private and public conduct. Otherwise, he could generally disregard the restraints of law, morality and popular opinion. Such calculations of power balancing and the requirements of political survival often generated short-lived alliance. The warlord thus had little concern for the systematic protection of his subordinates' rights, physical welfare, or career equity. A commander might impose punishments ranging from beating to death, without benefit of trial. In the better warlord armies, where a concern for dependent welfare

[4] Bland, *China, Japan and Korea*.

stood in stark contrast to the more generalised disregard for any reliable pay system, an illiterate soldiery was forced to accept occasional opportunities for looting as the principal reward for service.[5]

What of the warlords' effectiveness as military commanders, the ultimate criterion by which their very appellation insists they be judged? The qualities of a commander are reflected in the conduct of his men. Foreign observers of the period generally thought the performance of Chinese troops poor, though there were exceptions. The men tended to fight — when they fought at all —- as individuals or small groups rather than as co-ordinated units. The lack of marksmanship was due to the fact that there was seldom enough spare ammunition to conduct live target practice. One warlord warned his men that it was 'immoral' to fire without aiming — but this could have made little difference.

The civil wars of 1924 and 1925 in north China were observed at first hand by Lawrence Impey, a war correspondent who accompanied the armies of the Northern warlords Marshal Wu Peifu and General Li Jinglin, a leading subordinate of Zhang's. Among his observations was a comment on 'the general shortage of officers when any practical work was being done':

> If it is a conference or a parade, the whole ground is cumbered with officers of all grades, all equally excited and all equally inefficient, but when it comes to handling a food convoy, an ammunition train, a battalion passing up the lines of communication, or a battery in action the officers are usually noticeable by their absence. The work seems to be carried out either by the sergeant and corporals or by a peculiar system of common consent on the part of the rank and file, which it must be admitted works very well on some occasions.[6]

[5] William W. Whitson with Chen-hsia Huang, *The Chinese High Command: A History of Communist Military Politics, 1927–72*, New York: Praeger, 1973, p. 10.

[6] Lawrence Impey, *The Chinese Army as a Military Force*, Tientsin: Tientsin Press, 1926, p. 17.

Impey considered that 'a foreign division' (he presumably had in mind European, American, or Japanese troops) would be 'equal to at least two and possibly three Chinese ones'. But at another point he remarks that if the Chinese soldiery were properly trained and motivated, they would be a formidable proposition for any enemy to take on.

The early 1920s were a period when methods of warfare had been revolutionized in the recent global conflict. Military aviation had been used for the first time, as had tanks. (Sutton designed a tracked, armoured vehicle based on a Caterpillar tractor, which he called 'the Skunk' because it fired two mortars out of its rear.) Cavalry was all but defunct from the effects of the machine-gun; so, often, was massed infantry attack. Warfare had become as much a matter of protecting and concealing one's soldiers as of overwhelming the enemy — a concept fairly close to traditional Chinese military tactics.

Field artillery — which had enabled Western armies to defeat large bodies of Chinese troops as long before as 1858 — was still, by 1924, inadequately understood and operated by Chinese gunners, though Impey noticed a marked improvement in 1925. There was hardly any fire-control (field telephones were a novelty), ammunition and spent shell-cases were sloppily handled, and the use of fuses barely appreciated. High explosive was fired when shrapnel should have been used, and vice versa.

The handling of the small number of aeroplanes at the disposal of the warlords in various parts of China was hopelessly inefficient, in the manner of both piloting and attack. When they had no bombs they would drop heavy objects like wooden beams, with little effect on the enemy on the ground. The aviators — who included some Russians — shunned dogfights, partly because there were few mounted machine-guns, and in some confrontations the pilots just shot at each other with automatic pistols. They were not trained to gather intelligence from the air and were incapable of taking photographs. Soldiers paid little heed to them, though later on bombing attacks greatly demoralized civilians. Civilians and troops alike rushed to the location of bomb explosions in order to gather fragments as souvenirs.

Equally bad was the use of rail transport — the single economic and technical factor which did the most to haul China into the twentieth century. Lines were extremely congested, and officers mercilessly persecuted railway signallers and shunters who — with the best will in the world — could not meet their impossible demands. (During the 1925 civil war, the up-line from Tientsin to Qinhuangdao was blocked by trains, while the down-line was practically unused. Loading and unloading were hopelessly inefficient.)

As always in Chinese armies, the troops were inadequately fed, unless they looted from civilians. Their staple diet in the Northern wars consisted of stale steamed bread and, occasionally, some vegetables. Meat, fish, and eggs were almost unknown. Cold-weather clothing was often unavailable, and the soldiers wore cloth shoes which turned their feet into raw wounds when they had to undertake forced marches.

Medical treatment for the wounded was almost nonexistent close to the lines, and many men died of their wounds while waiting to be shipped by rail to Peking or other big cities, where foreign mission doctors and Chinese nurses worked round the clock to save as many as they could. Despite all this, Impey prophetically concluded:

> As far as actual courage and determination are concerned the Chinese soldiery of today compares very unfavourably with those of other civilised countries, for the simple reason that they have been betrayed by their leaders so often and so callously that they have no conception of the meaning of the word patriotism, and can see no good reason for sticking it out to the last ditch, unless it happens, as with Wu P'ei-fu [Wu Peifu], that the officer in command is one of those rare exceptions who have won the respect and confidence of the rank

and file. If the day ever comes when the majority of the
officers of the Chinese army are of that type, we shall
behold a military force in the making which will aston-
ish the world.

The Traditional Chinese View of War

The Chinese are often credited with being the world's most
peaceable people, despising war and soldiers. There is a widely quoted Chinese aphorism that 'good iron is not used to
make nails, nor good men turned into soldiers.' This is a
great over-simplification. China has an ancient and impressive military history. She has her heroes and villains, bullies,
champions, famous stratagems and tricks, and great generals
and their followers loyal to the death. The Chinese were casting bronze weapons over 3,000 years ago and later adapted
iron to military purposes. They had elaborate war chariots
and disposed of siege and counter-siege equipment. The
Great Wall is the biggest fortification ever built by man.

The Chinese were also familiar in ancient times with the
concepts of chivalry and military ethics. One of their oldest
classic books, the *Zuo Zhuan*, records how two nobles meet
on the field of battle, and one shoots at the other but miss-
es. He is tensing his bow to shoot again, when his antagonist
reminds him: 'Not [to shoot] by turn is cowardly!'
Thereupon the other takes his arrow from the bowstring, and
is shot dead by his enemy.[7]

The philosopher Sun Zi, about whose life little is known,
wrote a classic treatise on the art of war, which is still rele-
vant today. His basic theory is that in warfare the good commander will do his best to avoid head-on confrontation with
the enemy, as this will deplete his own men even if he wins
the battle. Sun Zi's advice is that the commander should
deploy a variety of stratagems and feints, to deceive and

---

[7] Cited in *Chinese Ways in Warfare*, Frank A. Kierman Jr and John K.
Fairbank (eds.), Cambridge, Mass.: Harvard University Press, 1974, p. 43.

intimidate the enemy, attack him where he is weakest and always leave him an escape route. Mao Zedong's thinking was not greatly dissimilar to that of Sun Zi's on military affairs.

One of the classic periods of Chinese warfare is the struggle between Liu Bang, who founded the Western Han dynasty after a protracted war with his rival, Xiang Yu. This war was recorded in some detail by Sima Qian, the most famous of Chinese historians, who wrote at the end of the first century BC and the beginning of the first century AD. Sima Qian was not just a historian and a superb stylist but a moralist too, so that he has sometimes been called the 'Chinese Thucydides'.

Sima Qian loved to point out the lessons of ethics and morals, intelligence and stupidity, generosity and evil deeds, which history supplied. He comments thus, for instance, on Xiang Yu, who is regarded as a kind of romantic tragic hero:

> He was boastful and liked to show off. He stubbornly clung to his own views, and made light of tradition. He dreamed of becoming an absolute ruler, through attacking the empire and subjugating it. Even when he was killed, he still could not see clearly or take the blame. He said: 'Heaven has destroyed me. I made no mistakes in waging war.' How wrong-headed this was![8]

Despite his liking for morals, Sima Qian was a highly objective writer whose prose can stand up with the best of the Greeks and Romans. But he was by no means cold or indifferent to the affairs of men: he was condemned to castration for having defended a general who had incurred the Emperor's wrath by surrendering to the enemy.

The period of the Warring States (475–221 BC) also supplies abundant materials for historians and students of historiography. In that period — which produced Confucius and

[8] Sima Qian, *Shiji, Benji: Xiang Yu* (The Records of the Historian, Basic Annals, Xiang Yu).

most of the other classical Chinese philosophers — the concept of warfare is fascinatingly intertwined with ideas of statehood and statesmanship, and the devious means whereby the rulers of the feudal kingdoms of the day sought alliances or declared war on their neighbours. The politico-military situations chronicled by historians of this period bear somewhat striking resemblances to those of the warlord epoch in the twentieth century — not surprisingly, since the geographical configuration of the country has remained unchanged (except for some large alterations in the course of the Yellow River).

The major differences between the wars of those feudal states and the struggles of the later warlords is that the latter were played out more quickly, and the entire period lasted only a quarter of century, by comparison with the Warring States, whose conflicts dragged on over centuries. The brevity of the modern campaigns, compared with those of ancient times when a state's chief general might be away from the capital city for even fifteen years at a time, is explicable mainly in terms of the technology involved. The Chinese Revolution was only seven years old, and the warlords already locked in struggle, when the First World War came to an end and the world saw military technology tremendously advanced by 'necessity, the mother of invention'. The weaponry was more deadly and the means of transport motorized — to say nothing of advances in naval power and aviation. Of course these developments took time to trickle into China, but there was never any shortage of Western and Japanese adventurers eager and willing to find employment by modernizing the warlords' armies.

Though the Confucian scholars, or literati, who made up the ruling élite from the late third century BC until the early twentieth century, affected to despise war and soldiers, they nonetheless relied on the imperial armies for their own safety and authority (there was no civilian police force to speak of). Imperial power was in theory absolute in every part of the country, but in practice it was thoroughly decentralized, even in times of national crisis, invasion, or civil war, when local commanders, in consultation with their civilian counterpart, the mandarinate, would do what they thought best to cope with the situation. If they failed — and that might be because of ambiguous or nonsensical orders from the Court — they were disgraced or executed. If they succeeded, they might win big appointments and honours.

In retrospect it is astonishing how the civilian mandarinate, with its relatively small establishment, kept as firm a grip as it did on the administration of their various provinces, regions, or districts, where their military counterparts held the real physical power. Indeed, there were times, especially in the Tang dynasty, when links with the imperial court became so tenuous that the provincial military commanders in outlying parts — the so-called *jiedushi* or Imperial Overseers — acquired independence in all but name.

Doubtless it was the physical weakness of the civil authorities that lay at the root of the contempt in which the governing literati regarded military commanders, and the low opinion which the civilian population had of the soldiery: both were expressions of fear. It was assumed by all and sundry that if the military were not kept in their place, they would rebel, loot, rape, and burn. And the armies gave civilians ample reason for such fears in times of invasion, civil war, or breakdown of authority in a peasant uprising.

But set against this hostility to war and warriors is the natural feeling of admiration and trust which a commander enjoys if he happens to be good at his job, patriotic, and humane. The definition of 'humanity', it is true, was somewhat broad, and did not inhibit a victorious commander from torturing and executing his prisoners. On the other hand, he could win popular appeal by restraining his troops from looting and massacring people by the wayside when they were campaigning. The 'good general' is the military equivalent of the 'upright magistrate' found in Chinese fiction and lore.

Apart from admiration for the great warriors of past ages, there is also a popular tradition of qualified support for rebels and even bandits. This tradition is most clearly laid out in the mediaeval novel *The Water Margin*, of uncertain authorship, which glorified the deeds of a band of Song dynasty outlaws. Under the leadership of the hero Song Jiang, they robbed the rich and occasionally helped the poor. They performed huge feats of valour and ate enormous, meaty meals washed down with gallons of rice wine. Eventually, however, they accepted an imperial pardon and went off to fight on the emperor's behalf.

Apart from its superbly entertaining style, *The Water Margin* encapsulates many of the underlying assumptions about politics and war common to most Chinese people. One is that there will be no social justice if there is bad government at the top. Another is that it is excusable to rebel and take up arms against the dynasty if one's grievances are severe enough. A third is the importance attached to ruse and guile in warfare. A fourth is that there is not necessarily any moral blame attached to changing sides.

The issues dealt with in *The Water Margin* lie so deep in the Chinese consciousness that they were used by the leftist 'Gang of Four', led by Mao Zedong's widow Jiang Qing, as an allegory to attack the late Premier Zhou Enlai and Vice-Chairman Deng Xiaoping in the official Chinese press in 1975.

The warlords of the early twentieth century frequently identified themselves with the military heroes of the past. They followed the precepts of guile and deception perfected by previous great commanders. They got this knowledge, usually in boyhood, from the hundreds of popular story-books about heroes of bygone ages — in many cases it was all the education they received, and the chief incentive for an adventure-loving boy to learn Chinese characters. Some of these works are still highly popular and are printed and disseminated in huge numbers in China today, and lent out to children at kerbside libraries.

The Chinese soldier, having been given something to fight for, showed enormous mettle in the Anti-Japanese War, the civil war that followed the Second World War, and the Korean War. The identification of the armed forces with the cult of Mao in the Cultural Revolution period (1966–76) gave them a sense of duty in peacetime, too, and the dismantling of the Mao cult by his successors aroused strong opposition in the People's Liberation Army (PLA). It remains to be seen how the PLA will develop, both as a fighting force and as a national institution, following Deng Xiaoping's efforts to make it a smaller, more professional body of men with less involvement in politics.[9]

[9] This was written before the terrible involvement of the PLA in Peking in June 1989. For the role of the PLA in the Peking Massacre, see Timothy Brook, *Quelling the People: The Military Suppression of the Democracy Movement*, Toronto: Lester Publishing Ltd, 1992.

1   The Soldier Statesmen

Yuan Shikai and the New Army

MUCH OF THE credit for the modernization that had been achieved up until the 1911 Revolution must go to Yuan Shikai, who was appointed to supervise the training of the New Army.[1]

By the early years of the twentieth century, China had come a considerable distance towards forming a modern army with up-to-date equipment and training. This process had been pushed forward especially by the statesmen Li Hongzhang, Zhang Zhidong, and Yuan Shikai himself.

China's defeat in the war of 1894–5 with Japan, and the invasion of the allied relief force which liberated the besieged legations in Peking in 1900, were both powerful stimuli to self-strengthening and modernization. Knowledgeable accounts of the transition of the Chinese army from a pre-modern to a modern military force have been left by Western officers who were permitted to observe training, or who organized training courses, or fought against Chinese troops in 1900, or served as military attachés at their countries' legations. One of the most informative of these is *L'Armée Chinoise*, by General H. Frey.

The French officer notes that a salient feature of the old Chinese army was its 'massive decentralisation'. The most important parts of the imperial army were the so-called Green Standards, mostly composed of Han Chinese troops.

[1] There are two excellent biographies of Yuan Shikai in English: Jerome Ch'en, *Yuan Shih-k'ai, 1859–1916*, 2nd edn., London: George Allen & Unwin, 1961; and Ernest Young, *The Presidency of Yuan Shi-kai: Liberalism and Dictatorship in Early Republican China*, Ann Arbor: University of Michigan Press, 1977.

Main treaty ports and leased territories, with dates of opening.

The Green Standards were divided into two classes: the first was the internal guard divisions, which in normal times were more concerned with certain types of police work than with warfare (China had no regular police force until modern times). Their tasks included enforcement of tax collection, law and order in the streets, and so on, and their armament until late in the nineteenth century consisted mainly of spears, crossbows, longbows, and old-fashioned muskets.

The second class of Green Standards were the war divisions, which handled rapid-fire rifles (mostly Mausers) and increasingly received training and drill after the European fashion of the day. They were used as bodyguards for officials, militia, frontier guards, and so on. They were mostly volunteers and their strength was flexible, in that fresh troops could be recruited in time of need. They were organized on a provincial basis and fought principally in their provinces of recruitment. Thus in 1860 the Anglo–French invasion force fought mainly the provincial troops of northern Zhili (Hebei province) and in the war of 1894–5 Japanese troops fought only with units from Zhili and Manchuria. The other war divisions remained in their home provinces.

The rationale of this seemingly weak use of the imperial armies was perhaps twofold. Imperial dynasties which fell into decline were mostly overturned by military force. So it was in the interests of the reigning dynasty to accustom its officers and soldiers to believing that they had no business campaigning outside their home province, whilst the armies of the metropolitan province would serve as bodyguards for the imperial family and its top official. Secondly, Chinese soldiers were notorious for their dislike of fighting far from their home province and suffered from low morale as a result of homesickness.

However, from the 1860s on, the provinces did sometimes submit detachments to direct central control, replacing them with local recruitment. These out-of-province soldiers were known as 'braves' and had the Chinese character for 'valour' inscribed on their jerkins.

The Green Standards were thought to number between 600,000 and one million — a figure of startling vagueness which indicated very poor central control or even knowledge of the provincial armies, or which might reflect the exaggerated troop strengths reported by local and provincial commanders in order to siphon off the pay of non-existent soldiers.

The highest ranks were occupied by Tartar (Manchu, occasionally Mongol) princes. Others were graduates of military schools, and were despised by the civilian mandarinate whose members took higher degrees in literature and philosophy. The personal army of the Manchu sovereign consisted of the so-called Eight Banners, consisting of Manchus, Hans, and Mongols. Besides making up the defence corps for the capital, they could serve as reserve and reinforcements in war (some Imperial Bannermen fought the Allied relief force in 1900, and two years previously small detachments had tried to prevent the British occupation of Hong Kong's New Territories).

China's armed forces could not be converted into a modern army overnight, but a succession of strong men near the top of the political system had seen the need for modernization and had experimented with it. By the first decade of the twentieth century there were various regiments receiving up-to-date training — mostly at the hands of German instructors. These, it was hoped, would spread their influence on the 'ink-spot' principle, with the best-trained units acting as a kind of leaven throughout the country. In addition, modern military academies were being opened and developed.

In 1894 the acting governor-general of Nanking, Zhang Zhidong, invited a German training mission of twelve officers and twenty-four warrant officers to train a modern army there. Two years later Zhang was ordered by imperial edict to Wuchang as viceroy of Huguang (the provinces of Hubei and Hunan). Drawing on experience gained at Nanking, he set about training the new army for central China. This was divided — on the old pattern — into two divisions, one specially attached to the viceroy and responsible for his safety and authority, and the other for general duties, known simply as the Wuchang Division.

The viceregal army consisted of three infantry regiments, one artillery regiment of eight batteries, one battalion of sappers, and two companies of railway guards to a total of about 9,500 men. The Wuchang Division consisted of three infantry regiments, one artillery regiment, and various units for railway guard duties and police work, with one battalion charged with defending the safety of the foreigners in the treaty port of Hankou, adjacent to Wuchang.

In addition to the roughly 20,000 men making up these two divisions, the viceroy had at his command some 40,000 men who had received no training from European officers or warrant officers, though they were armed with Mauser repeating rifles. Scattered in this mass were a few European-trained battalions which were used as model training units. Old-style soldiers were stationed at various strongpoints in Hubei and Hunan.

Central to the formation of a modern army was the establishment of military schools and academies. Around the turn of the century several were set up — at Peking, Tientsin, Baoding, Canton, Ningbo, and Wuchang. In Manchuria there were three military preparatory schools whose graduates could work their way up through the ranks to become officers. It also became increasingly fashionable for Chinese cadets to receive some of their training in Japan, and retired Japanese officers sometimes put their experience at the disposal of provincial commanders for training purposes. Russian, British, and French instructors were in service with the Chinese army, as well as Germans.

With these new training schemes, the Chinese soldier became less of a joke than he had been in the nineteenth century when first faced with European training and armament. Chinese and Manchu soldiers were not deficient in valour: it took great courage to stand up to armies so tech-

nologically superior to one's own. But the terms of battle
were too uneven for valour to bring more reward than death
or maiming. Given proper training, the Chinese soldier
could cut an excellent figure. General Frey quotes from the
report of a French observer who watched artillery drill performed by a unit of the new Beiyang Army:[2]

> The movements are gone through with punctilious pre-
> cision. The various operations of setting up battery,
> from the assembly to the disassembly of parts, are carr-
> ied out in perfect order and with a great speed. These
> troops have an aptitude for manoeuvre of a high degree.
> As their German instructor said, each of these soldiers
> has powers of endurance to withstand any test and is a
> good shot. They have excellent eyesight and strong
> nerves. Out of 10,000 men in the Wuchang garrison,
> there are already 3,000 trained in all types of weapons
> who are equipped, armed, drilled and trained in the
> modern fashion — capable of matching themselves
> against an equal number of European troops if they are
> well led.[3]

Foreign observers felt that the Wuchang troops were good
at drill in close or open formation, their movements being
neat, brisk, and effected in complete silence. Firing discipline
was good, the men firing accurately and without haste, with
correct adjustment of the rear-sight for range. The Chinese
gunners could take cover behind the gun by squatting for
long periods — something which Europeans find painful.
Chinese engineers or sappers were considered highly competent with a natural affinity for the work. The cavalry,
however, left something to be desired, for the ponies were

---

[2] The New Army was established after the crushing defeat of the old
Chinese armed forces by the Japanese in 1895. The key figure in creating the
New Army was Yuan Shikai. After further reforms in the post-Boxer period,
the most northerly parts of the New Army became known as the Beiyang
Army. This army was virtually Yuan's own personal fighting force; even dur-
ing the periods when he was out of power, he retained control of it.

[3] General H. Frey, *L'Armée Chinoise*, Paris: Hachette, 1904, pp. 46–7.

overburdened by the rider's armament of lance, carbine, and sabre, but dressage was good. Installations at the garrison headquarters were found to be of a high standard. The kitchens were clean, infirmary up-to-date, magazines and bath-houses in good order. Each man had his own bed which consisted of the upper surface of a wooden box, with drawers in which his effects were arranged. Bedding consisted of a mat, two blankets, and a mosquito-net.

It is of interest that the Wuchang garrison inspected by foreign observers and found to be in such good order should have become, in 1911, the flashpoint for the Chinese Revolution.

But despite the good starts made at Wuchang, Nanking, and elsewhere, most Chinese armies remained rather primitive. 'In general, when warfare was unavoidable', writes American military historian William F. Whitson, 'a Chinese military commander of 1924 could expect to fight with weapons and at a speed approximating to American Civil War conditions. At one extreme, the well-equipped forces of the Manchurian warlord Chang Tso-lin [Zhang Zuolin] impressed Western professionals, such as the commander of British forces in China.' However, the general standard of weaponry at the disposition of other warlords ranged 'from primitive to non-existent'. A regiment of some 1,500 men might be lucky to have four First World War-era machine-guns, and a single field-piece, usually a 75 mm. Not enough weaponry was produced in China to meet all the warlords' needs, which forced them to scrounge around for anything they could get in the way of foreign-made arms, and this led to an inefficient assemblage of mutually incompatible systems, including muzzle-loaders, single-shot rifles, Mauser repeaters, and pistols. 'Armies were universally clad in flimsy, blue-grey uniforms, the only distinguishing mark being an arm band, a practice that facilitated changing sides when the need arose.'[4]

[4] William W. Whitson with Chen-hsia Huang, *The Chinese High Command: A History of Communist Military Politics, 1927–72*, New York: Praeger, 1973, p. 11.

Yuan — often called the 'father' of the warlord system — was born in Henan province in 1859, in a family which made sure he got a solid classical education. The strong, active boy was adopted by a general in the imperial army. His inability to pass the more advanced of the civil service examinations pointed him naturally in the direction of a military career, and as a young officer he was engaged in military training — a subject that lay close to his heart for the rest of his life.

While still only in his early twenties, Yuan was dispatched to Korea as an officer in a Chinese brigade which was to defend China's suzerainty over that country, then being challenged by Japan. He became an aide to the commander of the brigade and attracted favourable notice for his personal and professional bearing. The Korean crisis was settled by the simple expedient of exiling the pro-Japanese regent and supporting the pro-Chinese queen, but Yuan was to spend a total of twelve years in the country. The war of 1894–5 resulted in Japan's annexation of Korea, and Yuan returned to Peking, where he was given charge of the military modernization programme.

The war with Japan prompted the Chinese to speed up their modernization plan, for it was now clearer than ever that Mongolian bowmen, Manchu cavalry, and Chinese foot-soldiers armed with spears and out-of-date firearms were no match for the troops of the imperialists who seemed intent on carving up China's territory among themselves. Aside from weaponry, the army lacked modern training facilities, skilled advisers and instructors, medical and surgical support for the wounded, a modern, logistical system of supply, and countless other factors that distinguished the imperial army of old from the new national defence force planned by Yuan Shikai, which became known as the Beiyang (Northern) Army.

In 1899 Yuan was responsible for exposing the attempt by a group of reformers to use the authority of the Emperor to bring about badly needed changes in Chinese government and society, which were opposed by the ultra-conservative

Empress Dowager Cixi, the power behind the throne. For this he was further promoted and became increasingly influential in the government.

At this time the fanatically anti-foreign Boxer sect was gaining momentum and its adherents were roaming the country, attacking missionaries and Chinese Christian converts, in a semi-patriotic, semi-mystical orgy of violence. Though they proclaimed themselves loyal to the ruling dynasty, the Empress Dowager and her ministers and commanders were uncertain whether to suppress the Boxers or to turn their spearhead firmly against the foreigners, who were enriching themselves at China's expense and rapidly undermining the authority of the Manchus and the Chinese mandarinate.

In June 1900, the Legation Quarter in Peking, where the foreign diplomatic missions were located, came under siege by Boxers and by rather unenthusiastic imperial troops. The legation guards of different nationalities managed to hold off the besiegers until a joint international expedition finally succeeded in pushing its way up from Tientsin and freeing the foreigners. Cixi fled in disguise to north-west China. Yuan Shikai, meanwhile, had declined to take any decisive action against the Boxers but had none the less strengthened his position as Viceroy of Shandong, and was further promoted to be acting Viceroy of Zhili and Commissioner for North China Trade, a lucrative post. He fell into political disfavour in 1909, however, and retired to his estate in Henan.

Over the years Yuan had proceeded with his central interest of modernizing the army, and to a considerable extent he had achieved this. By setting up military colleges, bringing in foreign instructors, procuring modern armaments and, even more importantly, ensuring sufficient funding, he managed to create a professional military. By recruiting a higher calibre of soldier and introducing reasonable conditions, he engendered an *esprit de corps*. As a result, the overall standing of the military improved. But for the Manchus it was too late. Imperial troops at Wuchang, in central China, mutinied on 10 October 1911. Yuan was appointed commander-in-chief of the imperial task force that was rushed to the triple city of which Wuchang was part, and recaptured Hanyang and Hankou, the other cities of the conglomeration which the revolutionaries had taken.

Yuan was appointed premier in recognition of his decisive actions. He then proposed a ceasefire and talks with the rebels, and declared himself in favour of a constitutional monarchy for China. Negotiations were conducted at Nanking in December and later transferred to Shanghai on a bigger scale.

The revolutionaries led by Sun Yatsen, and based in the south, were mistrustful of Yuan, however, considering him ambitious and unscrupulous. This accelerated the division of China into 'revolutionary South' and 'reactionary North', which dominated the country's history for the next sixteen or seventeen years. In February, the Manchu court declared that it would 'hand over sovereignty to the people at large', and named Yuan Shikai as chief executive to unify the country and restore peace. Full of goodwill, Sun Yatsen resigned in favour of Yuan as provisional president, under a provisional constitution which had been drawn up hastily at Nanking.

For the next two years, Yuan was preoccupied with putting the country's finances on their feet through both domestic revenues and foreign loans. He was also strengthening his personal rule with a series of judicial and extra-judicial acts, including arrests and assassinations, which intimidated those members of the new National Assembly in Peking who were loyal to Sun Yatsen. Sun himself, disgusted with Yuan, called for a war to bring him down.

In July 1913 the 'second revolution' broke out. Several provincial warlords rebelled against Yuan's rule, but commanders loyal to him put the rising down within two months, so that his position was if anything strengthened. The influence of the Kuomintang was concomitantly weakened, and Duan Qirui, a hard-liner and conservative who believed in uniting China by force, became premier. The

National Assembly voted Yuan into the presidency and he was installed with great pomp and ceremony.

The American minister to Peking, Paul Reinsch, described Yuan thus: 'His expressive face, his quick gestures, his powerful neck and bullet head gave him the appearance of great energy. His eyes which were fine and clear, alive with interest and mobile, were always brightly alert. They fixed themselves on the visitors with keen penetration, yet never seemed hostile, they were always full of keen interest.'[5] Contemporary portraits of Yuan in his mid-fifties show a grave, judicious expression beneath the drooping moustache and tiny chin-beard, the Western epaulettes emphasizing the strength of his shoulders. All in all, he was a formidable man.

Although he was president of the new Republic, Yuan had scant regard for republican institutions. Reinsch recalled:

> He had no real conception of the Commonwealth principle of government. Nor of the true use and function of a parliament, particularly of parliamentary opposition. He accepted these things as necessary evils that must be held within as narrow limits as possible. 'As you see,' Yuan explained to me eagerly, with evident enjoyment of his own metaphor, 'the Chinese Republic is a very young baby. It must be nursed and kept from taking strong meat or potent medicines like those prescribed by foreign doctors.'[6]

One of Yuan's most important acts — and a cause of much trouble for China — was his amendment of the Provisional Constitution of 1912, which had been drawn up by the revolutionary leaders, on the grounds that it gave too much power to them. He banned the KMT itself in November 1913, and drafted constitutional rules ascribing sweeping powers to the head of state. He then turned to the onerous task of finding money to run the government. An obvious

[5] Paul S. Reinsch, *An American Diplomat in China*, New York: Doubleday, 1922, p. 1.

[6] Reinsch, *An American Diplomat*, p. 3.

source of funds was Japan, but Tokyo never gave anything for nothing. When the First World War broke out, the Japanese seized the German concessions in Shandong province and along the railway there. As China's weakness became more and more evident, Tokyo presented a list of twenty-one demands. These would give Japan near-colonial power over the Chinese administration, police and armed forces, territorial leases in southern Manchuria and Inner Mongolia, and control of important economic resources. The Chinese government managed to salvage the bare appearance of resistance, but there was a violent wave of popular discontent — a premonition of that which swept the country on 4 May 1919. China in fact saved herself from total Japanese domination by falling apart into warring provinces and groups of provinces, with the result that the Japanese had no real government to deal with except the various military rulers.

Economic decline and banditry in the countryside marked China's demoralization and increased subjugation to foreign power. Meanwhile Yuan pursued the craziest scheme imaginable for a 'republican' president: his self-proclamation as emperor and founding of a new dynasty to replace the Manchus. He carried out lavish ceremonial functions similar to those of the imperial period, including the imperial sacrifices to Heaven, for which he presented himself as an emperor:

> At dawn on the winter solstice, December 23 [1915], the president drove in an armoured car to the magnificent Temple of Heaven on the southern outskirts of Peking. The entire route was covered with yellow sand, as was customary for the imperial drive, and was lined three-deep with soldiers who had been stationed there in the biting cold since the evening before. At the southern gate of the temple, the president entered a vermilion coach, which carried him to the temple itself. ... Once inside he changed out of his field-marshall's uniform into the sacrificial robe and headgear. The robe was

royal purple, adorned with twelve circular dragon designs, and the headgear was an oblong board on a tight fitting cap, an ancient imperial design.[7]

In the last year of his life, Yuan relied increasingly on the support of military commanders in the capital and the provinces who could force his will through over widespread public opposition. Indeed his proposed self-proclamation as emperor could be seen as the vital moment in the emergence of the warlord system which persisted in China until 1928, and in the case of some provinces into the 1930s and even the 1940s. It was also the moment when the southern and south-western parts of the country mostly repudiated him and gave their support henceforward to Sun Yatsen's party, the Kuomintang. The movement came to be known as the National Protection (*huguo*) movement.

The first to rebel openly was General Cai E, the *dujun* of Yunnan, and by 1 January 1916 he had gathered enough support for his opposition to Yuan to be able to declare the independence of the province. Cai immediately invaded Sichuan province from where he could threaten those parts of central China still under Yuan's rule. Yuan postponed his enthronement, as the southern provinces of Guangxi and Guangdong declared independence. By March, Yuan could see he was beaten and began to back off his plan to found a new dynasty. In June 1916, he died a disappointed man. Reinsch described the funeral cortège:

The huge catafalque on which the body of Yuan lay was borne by a hundred men. It was covered with crimson silk, embroidered in gold. Throngs of white-clad mourners preceded the catafalque. The sons of Yuan walked under a white canopy. Heading the procession were twenty heralds, followed by three detachments of infantry, bearing their arms reversed and accompanied by brass bands. After the infantry came a band of Chinese musicians, flutes playing plaintive strains.

[7] Jerome Ch'en, *Yuan Shih-k'ai*, p. 163.

> Then came a large squadron of riders in old Chinese cos-
> tume, carrying banners. Then followed lancers escorting
> an empty state carriage; Buddhist monks beating drums
> and cymbals; the President's band; long lines of bearers
> with sacrificial vessels preceding the sedan chair in
> which was set the soul tablet of Yuan; men bearing the
> food offerings, the momentoes of Yuan's personal life,
> and the wreaths from the funeral ceremony. High offi-
> cials came next, on foot, wearing uniforms or frock-
> coats and top hats.
>
> The vast throngs that lined the route behind lines of
> troops looked on in respectful silence. There was no sign
> of grief, rather mute indifference.

The results of Yuan's rule for China were almost entirely negative. True, he had bestowed on her a relatively modern army, but that army soon split up into factions governed by warlords. He had done little to speed economic or techno-logical development in the civilian sector, and had merely increased the government's indebtedness with foreign loans. He had weakened the nation's morale and self-respect, and failed to stand up to the Japanese. In this sense, Yuan showed the outline profile of the warlords to come: arrogant, auto-cratic, short-sighted, and ostentatious.

Duan Qirui[8]

The transition from the imperial period to the warlord era was to a considerable extent dominated by major political issues which helped to split the country up into provinces, each with its own policies and its own army. The biggest issues in the years immediately following the 1911 Revolution were the adoption of a republican constitution and the abolition of the monarchy.

[8] There is no English-language biography of Duan Qirui. Much of the material in this section is based on the vastly informative study of Peking warlords, written by Tao Zhujin, *Beiyang junta tongzhi shiqi shihua* (An infor-mal history of the northern warlords), Peking: Sanlian Shudian, 1957–8.

Following the Revolution of 1911, Sun Yatsen guaranteed the Manchu royal family safety and the right to continue living in the Forbidden City, as well as a fixed income of four million Mexican dollars every year and retention of their noble titles. Though deprived of political power, the imperial family's continued and visible existence was a potential rallying point for monarchists and conservatives who disliked the revolution. And as in the case of Yuan Shikai, the existence of the institution of monarchy, albeit only constitutional monarchy, was so recent that it provided a tempting prize for usurpers and restorationists.

Another factor leading to conflict was the location of the serious revolutionary forces in the south of the country. The parliament set up in Peking proved more and more useless because of the proximity of strong military forces originally under the conservative Yuan Shikai's command, and the constitution promulgated at Nanking in 1912 was little more than a scrap of paper when it came to the actual running of the country. The parliament was weak and corrupt, and although intellectuals and revolutionaries had pinned high hopes on it, its members were bought with the greatest ease by whomsoever had the most funds and political ambitions.

Duan Qirui was a talented young officer in command of the artillery corps of Yuan Shikai's modern-style army. He distinguished himself in 1900 during the suppression of the Boxers (from their full name 'the righteous harmonious fists'), and in 1911 was sent south to attempt the suppression of the army mutineers at Wuhan. In the 1912 peace talks held at Nanking between the revolutionaries and the Peking government's envoys, of whom Duan was one, he personally declared in favour of the abdication of the Manchu Emperor (the boy Puyi). This led to his appointment as Minister for the Army in the northern republican government which was headed by Yuan Shikai, and he was subsequently governor of Hubei province in central China.

In his increasing isolation towards the end of his life, Yuan turned to Duan as a capable ally who could rally support. In

April 1916 he appointed Duan premier of the Peking government in succession to Xu Shichang, who had lasted no
more than a month and who now retired to the countryside
to immerse himself in poetry.

Though tough and authoritarian, Duan himself was no
great lover of public office. He had Buddhist inclinations
and liked a quiet life. He devolved much authority to his
subordinates and usually stood by their decisions. His chief
professional interest was in the training of soldiers, and he
held on to the Ministry of War while accepting the premiership. However, as premier, he demanded real power and he
prevailed on Yuan Shikai to adopt the cabinet style of
government, with discussion of major issues limited to a
small ruling élite, rather than the more open, consultative
form of government favoured by many of the reformers and
revolutionaries.

The new premier also wanted Yuan to give up the title of
Grand Marshal and put all military power in the hands of
the War Ministry. None the less, Duan stood in a pupil-
teacher relationship *vis-à-vis* Yuan, and this was considered
near-sacred in the Confucian world view, especially among
military men. He could not contemplate directly overthrow-
ing Yuan. But in a short while — doubtless shorter than
Duan realized — nature was about to come to his aid. In the
meanwhile he transferred to Peking a detachment of troops
loyal to him, to guard against any dangerous consequences
of Yuan's growing jealousy.

In June 1916 Yuan sensed his approaching end and called
Duan, the Northern warlord Xu Shichang, and other presti-
gious figures to receive his political testament. Xu tried to
reassure him that he would soon recover, adding somewhat
inconsistently: 'If there is something you want to say, perhaps it would be a good idea to see to it as soon as possible.'

Yuan managed to say only two words: 'The Constitution'.
His deathbed visitors could not be sure whether he was referring to the constitution adopted in 1912 (more accurately
known as the Provisional Constitution) or the revised ver-

sion drafted under Yuan in 1914. Yuan had struck out of the original constitution the provision that if the president were unable to fulfil his office, his role would be taken over by the vice-president. He had substituted the rule that the dying president should write down the names of three men and put them in a sealed box, which would be opened after his death, and one of the three would be elected.

Yuan died on 6 June 1916. When the sealed box was opened, the names of Xu Shichang, Li Yuanhong, and Duan Qirui were found in it. None wanted to stick his neck out by showing eagerness for the presidency. At the lying-in-state, Duan suggested to Li that he take the job, but Li was nervous about the idea. Duan consulted with his senior military commanders, but contrary to their general sentiment, forced the reluctant Li to accept the presidency. Perhaps he calculated that a weak and unpopular president (the northern commanders considered Li a Southerner and therefore not one of them) would be easier to manipulate.

It seemed to be Li's fate to have 'greatness thrust upon him'. As a politician he was reasonably honest. But the height of his prestige had been reached when he was commander of the Hubei provincial army and was prodded into the leadership of the 1911 Revolution. Since then he had been in and out of office at the behest of others and was never a strong leader.

What was Li like, this sometimes diffident, sometimes ambitious and irascible president *malgré lui*? His face was puffy and a shade truculent, and he wore a big handlebar moustache; his hair, only slightly balding, was close-cropped. He had two large warts between the eyebrows, and a double chin. Receiving an American writer, Grace Thompson Seton, he compared China's condition with that of 'America two centuries before'. He rose every day at 5.30 a.m. and retired at 9 or 9.30 p.m. His favourite recreations were walking, skating, riding, and tennis. He liked Chinese opera, but thought the modern stage worthless. He was a strong believer in universal education, especially for women, who in his view should have the vote only when they were sufficiently educated. On taking his leave of the American writer, he 'clicked his heels together in a military salute'.[9]

Miss Seton also visited the parliament buildings and left the following description:

> The House of Representatives is much larger than the Senate, having about five hundred seats. The ceiling is timbered and the walls kalsomined in pink and white. It has chandeliers of glass clusters and brass, ugly Western stuff, the whole room without a trace of the beautiful colours and decorations and picturesque lanterns of less material days. The action here was quicker; the custom of handclapping had been introduced to express approval; and many of the members wore stovepipe trousers and frock coats. Some pamphlets for the day were being distributed. Printed in black upon red paper, they lay upon the oaken desks like splashes of dragon's blood.[10]

Yuan Shikai was buried with enormous pomp, and Duan Qirui became the effective dictator of north China. But it was not his destiny to unify even that part of the country: the forces of disintegration were already at work, and it would take thirty-three years finally to overcome them.

Duan was an authoritarian ruler and was irritated by having to explain his actions to a state council and to President Li, who was not content to be merely a rubber stamp for Duan's policies. Most of all Li, who had tried to refuse the presidency but, having got it, wanted to exercise his proper role, insisted on taking an interest in military affairs and in relations with the various warlords. Duan is said to have exclaimed at one point: 'I ask him to sign things and put his seal on them, not to sit on my head!'

---

[9] Grace Thompson Seton, *Chinese Lanterns*, London: Bodley Head, 1924, p. 117.

[10] Seton, *Chinese Lanterns*, p. 136–7.

Duan refused to agree to Li's attendance at sessions of the State Council (a kind of extended cabinet). Eventually a compromise was worked out whereby all proceedings of the council would be reported to Li, and its members would have a meal at his residence every Friday. If the President disagreed with some decision of the council, he must tell the Premier (Duan) his reasons for objecting, and the measure would be passed back to the council for re-examination. On the other hand, the President was not permitted to put his seal on any measures not passed by the State Council. Thus Duan ensured his own control of state decrees and other measures, reducing Li to the role of a spectator.

The central political problem was that of the constitution. Although Li Yuanhong would have automatically become president on Yuan's death under the 1912 provisional version, because he was vice-president when Yuan died, and although the 'sealed box' method achieved the same end by different means, the appointment was still, technically speaking, invalid, because no electoral body had been convened to choose between Li, Duan, and Xu. This indicated the contempt in which Duan, like Yuan Shikai before him, held constitutional reform.

One might have thought that for a country on the brink of disintegration and more than three decades of war, both civil and international, the question of the manner of Li's appointment was relatively trivial. But one must remember that at that time China had only five years' experience of the most tentative republicanism, in which 'democracy' had played only a tiny role. Yuan had revised the constitution, and Duan opposed any further change to it on the grounds that to tamper with it was the road to anarchy.

The Southern faction in Canton, including the prominent reformer Liang Qichao, demanded that the 1912 constitution be taken as definitive, otherwise Li Yuanhong's appointment as president must be declared invalid, and the State Council illegal. The arguments were hair-splitting; the basic conflict was the contention for power between Duan and the northern commanders on the one hand, and the southern constitutionalists on the other. Duan saw the constitution, any constitution, as desirable only if it increased his control, whilst the Southerners were anxious to use the constitution to prevent another bout of one-man rule such as that of Yuan Shikai.

On top of this, Yuan had illegally dismissed the parliament; if the old constitution were to be restored — parliament was dominated by the Kuomintang — its reconvention would threaten the authority of the northern warlords. Under the original constitution the parliament had a term of three years, so that the delegates of the 1913 parliament could claim they were illegally suspended in 1914 and should sit for another two years from the date of their restitution. Not everyone agreed with this. However there did seem to be a dominant trend of public opinion to the effect that the 1912 constitution should be reinstated and the parliament reconvened — a trend resisted mainly by the northern militarists.

On 15 June 1917, the commander of the First Fleet, Admiral Li Tingxin, who was based at Shanghai, with other top naval commanders, issued a statement supporting the old constitution and threatening to ignore any orders from Peking if it were not reinstated. They declared their alliance with the 'National Protection Army' of the south-west. This was a serious crisis for Duan, for although the navy only had three fleets, the First Fleet was the most important. Only the Second Fleet, which patrolled the Yangtze River and whose commander had close links with the northern warlords, had not sided with the Southerners. In the end Duan yielded to pressure, despite the reservations of most of the northern military commanders, and recalled the 1912 parliament in August 1916; less than a year later it was dissolved in the aftermath of General Zhang Xun's attempt to reinstate the Manchu dynasty. The original Provisional Constitution remained in force in Peking from 1916, when it was reinstated, until 1928.

An important task facing Duan in 1917 was the reduction in size of the various armies, either local, or with pretension to a national role, which had grown up in the confusion of the six years since the Wuhan revolution. This brought him into immediate conflict with other commanders and warlords, who were by now autonomous or semi-autonomous in their areas of command and unwilling to go back to taking orders solely from Peking.

He was backed by President Li, who was in favour of across-the-board troop-strength cuts all over the country. Duan, on the other hand, wanted to reduce the power of the most rebellious commanders in the south and south-west. Many of the Northerners were his friends or classmates, and naturally he did not want confrontation with them while the country was split on north–south lines.

Duan's plan was for an army consisting of forty divisions of 10,000 men each, as well as twenty independent brigades each of 5,000 men, to a total of 500,000. In addition, each province would supply local garrison troops to a total of not more than 200 battalions nation-wide. Each battalion would have a strength of 5,000 men, making a total of 100,000 provincial troops. This was based on the Qing system of 'a strong trunk with weak branches' inherited by Yuan Shikai, in which only the main-force divisions were mobile throughout the whole country and the provincial armies did not go beyond their boundaries. This was actually the opposite of what ensued in the warlord period, when local armies fought from one end of the country to another, and it was impossible to say which if any was the real 'national' army.

The splitting up of the armed forces from 1911 on meant that one province's troops might be incorporated into such-and-such a division operating on a regional basis. Or they might stay at home, or invade a neighbouring province. By the 1920s many a province behaved almost like a European country in military affairs, defeating or being defeated by others, imposing or suffering occupation, forming alliances or stabbing their allies in the back. The one stable rule was that the farther Chinese troops went from their home province, the less effective they were and the more demoralized they became. So despite the centrifugal tendency of national disintegration, there was also the centripetal tendency felt by troops and commanders for their home province. The advantage of single-province recruitment, or recruitment from two or three adjacent provinces, was that the men generally understood each other's dialects, and shared customs, superstitions, tastes in food, and so on.

Duan's plan to weaken the regional and provincial warlords, especially in the south, and to force the south to agree to disarmament seemed impossible unless he could defeat its troops on the battlefield. Those independent provinces were withholding taxes from Peking in order to build up their own forces. They were also fighting among themselves, with Yunnan and Guizhou contending for control of Sichuan. Guangxi and Guangdong were also intermittently at war or occupying each other's territory.

Duan Qirui ran into serious trouble in the first half of 1917 when the British and American ministers pressed him to sever relations with Germany and declare war on that country. Chinese opinion was split. To enter the war, without necessarily sending any troops to Europe, might ensure China a seat at the inevitable peace conference and give her a chance to stand up for her own rights usurped by the Powers. Japan was already allied with Britain, France, and Russia, though her action had been mainly limited to grabbing Qingdao in Shandong province and the railway from there to the provincial capital of Jinan from the Germans in 1914. Actually Japan was not especially in favour of China joining the Allies: it would hamper Tokyo's plans for greater domination of China in the post-war period. But on 10 March Duan addressed the parliament and urged it to sanction the break with Germany; the very least benefit he could expect would be loans from the Allies. Parliament wavered, and nearly the whole of Duan's cabinet resigned. Mobs were out on the streets, probably instigated by Duan to intimidate the members of parliament. President Li took it upon himself to dismiss Duan in May — a signal turning point in their respective fortunes.

In April 1917, Zhang Xun, a veteran commander loyal to the Manchus, occupied Peking, and on 1 July re-enthroned the boy emperor Aisin Gioro 'Henry' Puyi, proclaiming the restoration of the Manchu dynasty. President Li immediately restored Duan Qirui, who was in Tientsin, to the premiership. Zhang Xun, nicknamed 'the pigtailed general' by foreigners because he and his men retained their queues instead of cutting them off after the 1911 Revolution, was routed in a few days by forces loyal to Duan, who thereafter consented to emerge from retirement as premier.

Zhang escaped with some of his troops to the grounds of the Temple of Heaven, where he began negotiating with the Northern Republican forces under Duan. Eventually their positions were stormed and the restoration — which the young Emperor 'Henry' Puyi had not particularly wanted — was at an end. Li Yuanhong resigned as president and was replaced by Feng Guochang, the governor of Jiangsu. Duan returned to his old job as premier and to his self-appointed task of 'unifying China by force'.

The strongest military opposition to Duan's government was in the south-western provinces of Yunnan and Guizhou. His original plan had been to attack them through Sichuan, and then to thrust through Yunnan into revolutionary Guangdong and Guangxi. But Hunan's army was relatively weak, and it was closer to Peking than the other rebellious provinces; it could be attacked via Hubei and Jiangxi, so in the end Duan decided to take this easier route, rather than the arduous trek via Sichuan across high mountains and swift rivers. He estimated that he could subdue the southwest within five months at the outside.

The *dujun* of Hunan was the cultivated Tan Yankai, whose authority was somewhat shaky though he had useful connections among the military group controlling Guangxi province to the south-west. He tried to arouse the people of

Hunan to active opposition to the Northern warlords, using the slogan 'Hunan people should rule Hunan'. In Peking, Duan countered by sending a Hunan-born commander, Fu Liangzuo, to act as *dujun*, whilst Tan would be civil governor only.

Without formally opposing Fu, Tan appealed for help to the Guangxi warlord Lu Rongting, who contacted Peking and suggested that Hunan be regarded as a neutral zone to prevent a north–south war. The Yunnan warlord Tang Jiyao suggested sending Yunnanese troops at present stationed in Guangdong to help Hunan, and Lu agreed to this, quoting the famous Chinese proverb that 'if the lips are removed, the teeth will be cold' — the lips in this metaphor representing Hunan, and the teeth Guangdong and the south-west.

However, the south-western troops could not reach Hunan in time to resist the Northerners, so Tan Yankai took the line of least resistance and formally welcomed Fu Liangzuo to the province. Meanwhile he sold off some of the property of the provincial government and gave all his civil and military officials an extra month's pay to assure himself of their loyalty. Many lower-ranking officials wrote letters of resignation, to impress Peking with their loyalty to Tan. A string of farewell banquets was arranged in his honour, giving the impression that he would not consent to act as civil governor without military power. It was widely expected in Changsha, the provincial capital of Hunan, that Fu's appointment would be short-lived and Tan would make a comeback. Tan indeed soon declared his autonomy in southern Hunan.

Just as the supporters of Duan's pro-war policy had coalesced into a loose group of military commanders known as the 'Anfu Group', the recurring polarization of Chinese politics brought reaction — the tightening of ranks among other commanders which resulted in the formation of the 'Zhili Clique' (I prefer the terms Zhili Group and Anfu Group). Zhili province, roughly equivalent to modern Hebei, completely surrounded Peking municipality. It stretched north to beyond the Great Wall and had a major seaport, Qinhuangdao, on the Gulf of Bohai, then called the Gulf of Zhili. President Feng Guochang was regarded as the major figure of the Zhili Group, but living as he did in Peking, his freedom of action against Duan and his Anfu allies was limited.

The Anfu and Zhili groups often overrode considerations of geography, and were somewhat fluid in composition. An officer commanding a garrison might be considered to belong to one faction, but he could be swayed to the other by venality, revenge-seeking, family ties, loyalty to a former teacher, or pique at having been passed over for promotion. The central location of the Anfu Group was in Peking, but the Zhili Group did not have a fixed capital: the headquarters of the faction was wherever the strongest pro-Zhili commanders were present. Usually this was Baoding, the provincial capital.

Five strong outside pressures affected the Anfu and Zhili groups and their relations with each other. One was the army of the Christian General Feng Yuxiang, which was peripatetic and shifting in its alliances. Another was Japan, which had already begun the process of encroachment in Manchuria. Another was the army of the Manchurian warlord Zhang Zuolin. There was also the threat from the south and southwest, where the revolutionary forces loyal to Dr Sun Yatsen were located. And there was the constant danger of military intervention on the coast or along the Yangtze by the Great Powers, notably Britain.

The independent provinces in the south-west were hoping that the Zhili Group, through President Feng, would stop Premier Duan's Anfu Group of military commanders from invading Hunan further and threatening the south and south-west. Lu Rongting, the *dujun* of Guangxi, was trying to persuade the Chinese navy to come to the aid of the South-west and prevent the Northerners from conquering Hunan and Guangdong and 'watering their horses in the Pearl River' (on which Canton stands). Lu also denounced Premier Duan for his friendly relations with the Japanese. He demanded that Li Yuanhong be restored to the presidency in preference to Feng Guochang. He also wanted Duan to be dismissed from office and General Fu Liangzuo's forces to be withdrawn from Hunan.

The Anfu Group were infuriated by the defiant stand of the South-west, and Duan promptly borrowed money from Japan to enable him to fulfil his ambition of defeating Guangdong, Guangxi, Guizhou, and Yunnan and re-uniting China by force. The new President Feng Guochang was loth to 'dismiss' the rebellious *dujun* Lu Rongting from his posts in Guangxi — which were anyway not in his gift, as Guangxi considered itself independent. But he eventually put the presidential seal on the dismissal, under direct pressure from Duan. Meanwhile the south-western provinces realized war was inevitable, and they stepped up their contacts with Canton in the interests of forming an effective alliance.

The province of Hunan is not ideal for warfare. It is hilly and has a wet, almost sub-tropical climate. It has a history of poverty and rebellions. The people (like their most famous son, Mao Zedong) speak a dialect incomprehensible to other Chinese. It is the most direct route from the north into southern China as its boundaries adjoin Hubei, Sichuan, Guangdong, Jiangxi, and Guizhou. The people are known as clannish and hot-tempered, thriving on hot chillies.

The fighting developed in unexpected directions. Wang Ruxian, commander of the North's Eighth Division, suddenly proposed a ceasefire in Hunan. Fu Liangzuo fled the provincial capital, Changsha, by river boat. The local people acclaimed Wang, and he seemed to be grooming himself as provincial *dujun* — an extraordinary impertinence from Premier Duan's point of view. The Eighth Division was a crack unit, which had helped put down the Pigtailed General Zhang Xun's bid to restore the Manchu dynasty, and was thought one of the least likely to mutiny against Peking. But Wang Ruxian had contacts with the Zhili Group, and clearly was ambitious. Duan had made a big mistake by putting him in command. His troops included some who had been inducted from General Zhang Xun's defeated forces after the Manchu restoration attempt. They did not want to come to south China and did not want to fight: they felt they had been cheated. They went on strike for rations, they deserted and defected. It made sense for Wang to grab what he could and proclaim a ceasefire, though he might one day face the wrath of Premier Duan.

On 16 November 1917, Duan sent out an open telegram in which he painfully declared his resignation in the interests of Northern unity. He said that when he had previously resigned in May 1917, he had intended to shut himself up in his house and refuse to receive visitors. He had been forced to return to office to form a new cabinet. His dispatch of troops to fight in Hunan, he said, was purely in the interests of protecting the North and uniting the whole country. As to events on the Hunan front, they were caused by 'treacherous agitators'. He had been very distressed to realize that among his colleagues there were those who refused to consider 'the good of the nation as a whole', and who could bring disaster on China. Duan defended his own strategy of uniting China by force, saying that the country was in a state of collapse, and only 'we Northerners' had the power to save it, and to 'defend the constitution' (a document for which Duan and his friends had never shown any great respect).

President Feng Guochang began the hunt for a politician suitable to act as premier following Duan's resignation. Calculating that the anti-war commanders in the North were more numerous than the pro-war faction, he believed that in conjunction with the weight of his own office, it should be possible to avert further hostilities. He approached several prominent politicians, but none dared throw himself into the surf of the Hunan crisis.

On the day Duan resigned, the cabinet's Japanese adviser, General Aoki, visited President Feng and warned him that with the intensification of the war in Europe, Japan would look askance at political instability in China, and could not remain indifferent to it. The Japanese ambassador gave Feng a similar warning. Feng was alarmed by these signs of Japanese support for Duan, which would counter-balance Zhili's superiority in numbers.

While the problem of the premiership remained unsolved, President Feng used his constitutional powers to strip Duan of his military command, which he, Feng, thought should belong to himself. But for reasons of caution he transferred it instead to Wang Shizhen, a former member of Yuan Shikai's entourage, and asked him to form a cabinet. Xu Shucheng was made Deputy Commander in Chief — a strange bedfellow for Wang, who had once dismissed him from the War Ministry for embezzlement. The chain of command now went from Feng through Wang to Xu, and the last-named was soon shuttling back and forth by train between Peking and the Hunan front, reporting, investigating, and seeing to the implementation of orders. To complete his control of the military, President Feng moved the general staff from the premier's office to his own. Duan indirectly criticized these changes but was powerless to prevent them.

When Wang Shizhen had organized a cabinet, several main Northern commanders conferred in Tientsin and decided to make a two-pronged attack on Hunan using 200,000 men, despite the opposition to the war on the part of President Feng and the Zhili Group which controlled the Lower Yangzi. Reluctantly, Feng issued the order for the attack. The South-west called for a ceasefire. The commanders of the three Yangzi provinces declared their frontiers closed to other armies. The split between the Zhili and Anfu groups was now explicit, with President Feng trapped between them.

In March 1918, however, the Northern politicians and commanders settled their differences sufficiently to invite Duan Qirui to return and organize a new cabinet. Duan had probably known this would happen when he resigned, because there simply was nobody more competent then he.

Feng was forced to swear loyalty to his old rival and return to him the powers of military command which he had seized during Duan's absence.

Duan now drew up plans for simultaneous attacks on Hunan, Sichuan, and Guangdong. The Yangtze warlords had lowered their protesting voices when the formidable Duan returned to power. There was pressure within the Anfu Group for the overthrow of President Feng. But in the shifting tides of Peking politics, it was more difficult to arrange something than to plot it; the situation had a certain amount of inertia.

The one gaining most in all these tidal flows was Xu Shucheng, nicknamed Little Xu. He enjoyed Duan's full confidence, and brought the army's general staff under his own control, dismissing the previous incumbent as well as the head of the president's secretariat.

Although Duan's prestige was high when he was out of office, as soon as he returned he was beset by demands for military provisions and munitions, and those making the greatest clamour were the pro-war Anfu leaders who pushed him back into office. A shipment of arms from Japan was intercepted by Manchurian troops at Tanggu, the port of Tientsin, but Duan did not dare to make an issue of it, hoping to win an alliance with Marshal Zhang Zuolin, the Manchurian overlord. The Northern troops in Hunan were making very slow progress, which they explained on the grounds that they were short of supplies.

Duan decided to convene a large military conference in Hankou in Wuhan, to reconcile the Anfu and Zhili groups and forge a new unity among the Northern commanders. As things were, enthusiasm for the war was distinctly lacking, and the commanders and men were unsure of the likely success of a full-scale drive against the south and south-west.

Duan's conference misfired. Four of the main commanders — Li Chun of Jiangsu, Chen Guangyuan of Jiangxi, Zhang Jingyao, commander of the Northern Seventh Division, and Zhang Huaizhi, *dujun* of Shandong and com-

mander of the Second Route Army — failed to turn up on the
grounds that they had too many military duties to attend to.
Probably they were afraid of putting themselves in the power
of Duan and his rival, Cao Kun, who might use the opportunity to settle old scores. In the end Duan persuaded Zhang
Huaizhi to show up. The conference was attended by Duan's
senior staff officers from Peking but only by representatives
of the *dujuns* of Jiangsu, Jiangxi, Hunan, Anhui, Shanxi and
Fengtian (Manchuria). Their commanders stayed at home.

Duan addressed the Hankou conference on the importance of unity and the need for an assault on the south. He
outlined the coming campaign — the fourth against Hunan
— and gave appropriate instructions to the commanders.
Duan also expressed much goodwill towards the Zhili-
aligned warlords, and took several measures designed to
please them. The most important was his agreement to hold
elections for a new parliament to replace the Provisional
National Council. While Premier Duan was at Hankou, his
office in Peking received numerous telegrams from all over
the country opposing the war in Hunan and denouncing
him for carrying on secret diplomacy with Japan. President
Feng, doubtless with glee, sent these down the line to him to
deal with.

In May, public bodies and associations of merchants in
Wuhan, of which Hankou was a part, bombarded Duan with
demands for audiences to express their hostility to the war,
but he snubbed them. On 25 May he left Hankou to return
to Peking, calling in on Li Chun, one of the *dujuns* who had
refused to come to Hankou, at Nanking on the way.
Misfortune dogged his steps. The gunboat he was travelling
on collided with a passenger ferry and 700 people were
drowned, the soldiers on Duan's ship stabbing with bayonets
anyone in the water who tried to clamber aboard. Duan continued his journey by switching to another warship.

With the Hunan campaign stalled in mid–1918, anti-war
sentiment was growing in the Northern armies, and even the
pro-war *dujun* of Anhui, Ni Sichong, wanted to withdraw his

troops to rest them. Duan and Xu's last chance of winning in Hunan was to persuade the able Marshal Wu Peifu to continue the fight. He knew that Cao Kun had been taking the credit for Wu's victories, which were practically the only bright spot in the campaign. Finally disgusted with the protracted war, Cao Kun returned to Baoding to sit it out. Zhang Huaizhi went home to Shandong. Before leaving Hankou, both men sent out a telegram calling for a ceasefire in Hunan. Duan refused to believe the telegram was authentic, but he now understood the strength of the pro-peace faction, which had made serious inroads among the Northern commanders.

Dissension grew as five brigade commanders demanded a ceasefire and staged a kind of military go-slow. A joint appeal from all the Zhili commanders (except Wu Peifu) said that Hunan had suffered severe flooding, epidemics were raging, and the soldiers were too tired to go on fighting. The ferocity of some of the troops from the north had alienated the people of Hunan, and served warning on Guangdong and Guangxi with what to expect if they failed to unite and resist the invasion. Duan offered the Southern armies the option of joining up with the Northerners with their present ranks, or being paid off and dispersing. But his troops' performance had not been good enough to win over the Southerners, whose mistrust of Northerners was proverbial.

An attempt to divert Guangdong's attention from the Hunan front by invading the province from Fujian had been a failure. The combined forces of Fujian and Zhejiang had taken a beating from the troops of the Guangdong *dujun* Chen Jiongming, a relatively enlightened educationalist and reformer who had come to military command late in life but shown talent for arms. He smashed the invasion force and counter-attacked into Zhejiang.

The elections held in August 1918 were marked by every form of cheating and malpractice. The first-stage elections for the house were characterized by the British Consul at Nanjing, Bertram Giles, as 'a veritable orgie [sic] of corruption and rowdyism'. He wrote: 'The quotations for votes and the daily market fluctuations were chronicled in the native press as that of a marketable commodity, on the same footing as rice or beancake or other articles of commerce.' It was not unusual for an election supervisor to retain a large block of tickets that should have been handed out to registered voters, fill in the names of fictitious voters, and drop them into the ballot box or hire 'beggars, hawkers, fortune-tellers, peasants and such small fry' to cast their votes. Alternatively, the election deputy could sell a packet of tickets to a candidate who would proceed the same way. Some candidates, unable to buy enough tickets, hired toughs to seize them at the polling booth. In some cases, one candidate paid the other to withdraw.[11]

Duan now unveiled a new campaign plan for Hunan. This entailed 'holding' Hunan (which his forces did not yet even wholly control) and attacking through that province into Guangdong. Duan calculated that with 45,000 men he could take Canton in two weeks, and threatened to kill any member of parliament he found there, on grounds of treason. His threats were empty. His design for reunification by force had essentially failed, and although Duan hung on for a while longer, he was increasingly upstaged by two major commanders — Zhang Zuolin in Manchuria, and Wu Peifu in central China. The last part of Duan's career will be told through the careers of the men who helped to bring him down.

At the Versailles peace conference following the First World War, China's delegates failed to obtain the return of the territory formerly occupied by Germany in Shandong province, which was assigned instead to Japan. On 4 May 1919 this decision unleashed a flood of demonstrations and protests by millions of Chinese — students, writers, teachers, and merchants. The seething tide of public opinion concerning the Allies' shabby treatment of China demonstrated

---

[11] Foreign Office document, cited in J. K. Fairbank, ed., *The Cambridge History of China*, Vol. 12, Cambridge University Press, 1993, p. 275.

a new form of Chinese patriotism, fuelled not just by old superstitions and hatred of foreigners, justified or not. It helped in the crystallization of an intelligent patriotism which found the West and Japan not only guilty of bullying China and stealing her territory, but also of rank hypocrisy in their dealings with her. China, at the urging of the United States and Britain, had broken relations with Germany in 1917. Admittedly only some Chinese labour battalions ever went to the war theatre in Europe; none the less China was politically committed to the Allies' overall cause. The May Fourth protests unified the expression of indignant public opinion regardless of rank or class, and consolidated the role of students in the making of political realities; Chinese students remained a force to be reckoned with.

The movement showed the warlords up: they were the only people capable of defending China's interests by force of arms, and they often cloaked their rapacity in patriotic slogans. The May Fourth movement exposed their feebleness and venality in coping with foreign powers, by comparison with their merciless bullying of their fellow Chinese. Duan's historical reputation is ignominious — determined as much by his reputation as the 'enemy' in the May Fourth protests as anything else.

2   The Northern Warlords

Zhang Zuolin

O F ALL REGIONS of China in the 1920s, Manchuria[1] was the most strategically important. If one looks at the map of China as resembling a seated goat, then Manchuria makes up the head and horn of the beast, with the Liaodong Peninsula as the beard. It consists of three provinces. Heilongjiang is the largest, with its long frontier with Russia, bounded on the north by the Amur River, and on the East by the Ussuri. To the south of Heilongjiang lies the province of Jilin, more commonly known in the West by its Japanese version, Kirin. To the south, Liaoning province lies like a bridge between Korea and the Chinese province of Zhili (Hebei) which surrounds Peking. Liaoning's capital is Shenyang, previously called Mukden.

In the warlord period Liaoning was known as Fengtian, but this appellation was also used to cover Manchuria as a political whole under the rule of Marshal Zhang Zuolin, which ended with his assassination by the Japanese in 1928. The region was sometimes (confusingly) called 'the three eastern provinces', whereas today it is commonly referred to just as 'the north-east'.

---

[1] I have mainly eschewed the use of the term Fengtian, which is unfamiliar to the majority of Western readers, and have instead referred throughout to Manchuria, except when dealing with one of the three provinces individually. By the 1920s, the Manchu as a recognizable nation were being rapidly absorbed by the Chinese, and by now very few speakers of the Manchu language are to be found in China. I use the word 'Manchurian' as a geographical term which should not necessarily be seen as indicating ethnicity.

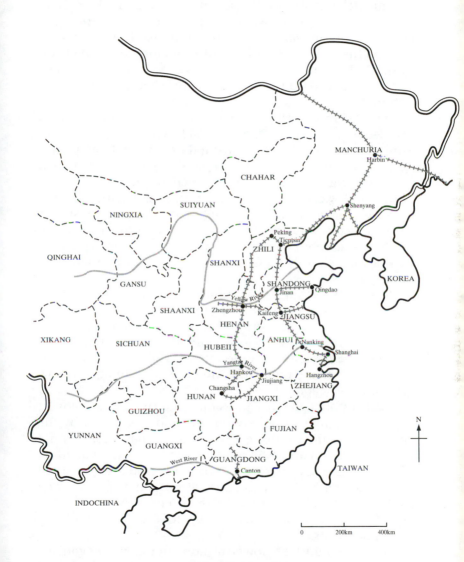

Main railway lines, 1926–7.

Though Manchuria has a harsh climate, with near-continental winter conditions, it is agriculturally rich in such hardy crops as wheat, millet, sorghum, and soya beans. There are large coal and iron-ore deposits, which enabled the Japanese to turn it into a major industrial region in the 1930s, when they established a puppet regime there. There is much pasturage for cattle, and the swift rivers are rich in fish.

The Manchus, a semi-nomadic people skilled in warfare, invaded and defeated China in 1644, destroying the native Ming dynasty. Under two outstandingly capable emperors, Kangxi (reigned 1662–1723) and Qianlong (reigned 1736–96), the Chinese empire reached the height of its power and wealth towards the late eighteenth century. However, the decadence of the Qing or Manchu dynasty in the nineteenth century was aggravated by conflicts with the Western seafaring powers and with the Russians, who were encroaching steadily on China's northern and Central Asian perimeter.

Most of Manchuria was underpopulated, the Manchu emperors having decided to keep their ancestral lands to themselves, but in the nineteenth century the immigration of Han Chinese settlers was permitted, to ease the growing population pressure in the heartland. The Hans, as they do everywhere, drained marshes and cleared pasturage to grow grain and vegetables.

Japan, with its growing power as a naval and land power, was increasingly casting envious eyes on Manchuria by the end of the nineteenth century. Japan had few natural resources and its domestic markets were limited. Manchuria offered both markets and resources to whomever was bold enough to grab it. To test her strength, Japan defeated China in the war of 1894–5, and a decade later fought the Russian Tsarist forces and sent their navy to the bottom of the Tsushima Straits.

Set in the midst of powerful and mutually antagonistic national interests, Manchuria has been variously styled 'cockpit of Asia' and 'the jewel of Asia'. In an age when most of the European powers and even America were scrambling for colonies and rights and concessions all over Asia, Japan could be forgiven for believing that its manifest destiny was in East Asia and that it had just as much, if not more, right to chew bits off China's carcass as anyone else. And with Europe heading for war and Russia for revolution, Japan's annexations in Manchuria were relatively easy to obtain.

Zhang Zuolin was a Manchurian village urchin nicknamed 'pimple', who by the end of his life ruled three Chinese provinces and disposed of vast wealth and power. Born into a poor family in Haicheng county of Liaoning province, the southernmost province of Manchuria, he spent his early youth fishing, gambling, and brawling. When he decided to earn some money he took a job as an ostler and waiter at an inn, where he listened avidly to the tales of the bandit gangs that infested north-east China. The only useful thing he learnt was a smattering of veterinary science. In 1896 he joined a well-known bandit gang, but four years later the Boxer Rebellion broke out and his gang joined the imperial army. Later he acted as an escort for travelling merchants. In the war between Russia and Japan in 1904–5, he favoured the Japanese who were fighting the Russians on Chinese soil in Manchuria. After that he became a cavalryman serving on border patrol and bandit- suppression duties.

When the 1911 Revolution occurred, some commanders in Manchuria wanted to seize the opportunity to declare independence for the three north-eastern provinces. The pro-Manchu governor used Zhang and his men to keep control of the situation and set up a 'Manchurian People's Peacekeeping Council'. The governor attended the inaugural meeting in Mukden (now Shenyang), the provincial capital, but was shouted down by a revolutionary, whereupon Zhang and his cronies drew their pistols and the meeting dispersed. The governor declared the council established, with himself at its head, and Zhang as Vice Minister of Military Affairs. Zhang brought about 2,500 men into Mukden to prevent civil disturbances. The revolutionary movement in Manchuria was severely set back, and Zhang, through his show of loyalty, enjoyed an enormous promotion.

On 1 January 1912, Sun Yatsen was inaugurated as president of the Chinese Republic in Nanking. Yuan Shikai in Peking secretly ordered his subordinate commanders to send telegrams opposing Sun's appointment. He promised to reward Zhang Zuolin when the situation had settled down, and sent him a substantial amount of military provisions, whereupon Zhang sent Yuan a huge and precious ginseng root epitomizing their close relations. Zhang then murdered a number of pro-revolutionary figures in Mukden and was rewarded with high-sounding titles by the near-defunct Manchu court. When he saw that Yuan Shikai was setting himself up as the national leader, he gave him his support and turned his back on the Manchus.

In June 1912, the general dissatisfaction and shortage of supplies for the Mukden garrison led to an armed uprising, which brought from Tokyo the threat that Japanese troops would intervene to protect their nationals. Zhang succeeded in putting down the somewhat aimless rebellion, and this strengthened his control of the city. Yuan Shikai, impressed by Zhang's firmness, renamed the troops under his command as the Seventh Division, and raised him to the rank of lieutenant-general. Zhang's ambition, however, reached way beyond this promotion; he dreamed of ruling all Manchuria, a prize that would indeed soon be in his grasp.

Zhang cultivated friendly relations with the Japanese who controlled the region around Dalian and Port Arthur as the base-territory for their Kwantung Army set up in 1905, an area of more than 3,400 square kilometres. The Japanese also controlled the South Manchurian Railway between Dalian and Changchun, and stationed troops along it. (Both concessions had been extracted from China in 1905, after the Japanese victory over the Tsarist Russian forces: the land war had been fought exclusively in Chinese territory; at sea, Japan destroyed the Russian fleet, her first major victory over a great power.)

Though he did not like so much Japanese influence in Manchuria, Zhang was realistic enough to be aware that he could not control the region without some co-operation from Japan. At the same time he was playing a cat-and-mouse game with Yuan Shikai. Though he deprecated himself as a political dunce, and affected to be a military man pure and simple, he was actually very astute, indeed cunning. When Yuan praised him for his work in bandit-suppression, he used this as a pretext to buy machine-guns and train squads in their use, and to ask for more supplies from Peking. Yuan did not, however, always accommodate him.

In 1913, suspicious of Zhang's ambitions, Yuan tried to move him to a position of authority in Mongolia, but Zhang sent him a reproachful telegram, recalling that he, Zhang, had kept order in north-east China while Yuan was trying to quash the revolution in the south.

When war broke out in Europe, China stood on the side-lines. Zhang's power in Manchuria had grown to the point where he could go lobbying for his own interests in Peking. When visiting the capital in 1915, however, Zhang made an elaborate display of submission to Yuan's authority, and was honoured by Yuan in return. In the play-acting of Chinese politics, any educated person could see that Zhang was putting himself in a special role — that of the loyal subject with no political ambition — and it therefore was incumbent on Yuan to show that he accepted this ploy at its face-value, though everyone knew he did not. This was a fine example of the Chinese taste for theatrics in politics; by putting himself out no end, Zhang forced Yuan to pretend to trust him. It was, indeed, the opposite of the Western game of 'life-manship' or 'one-upmanship', in which the goal is to demonstrate one's superiority as subtly as possible. In China it was a tactical victory to show one's humility, as long as the demonstration did not go beyond the bounds of 'face-sav-ing'. The result of all this parleying, bowing and scraping, and mouthing of insincere compliments was frequently a bloody civil war or an assassination.

Yuan's own ambition was now directed towards the restoration of the monarchy with himself as founder of a new dynasty. He solicited the opinions of senior military commanders throughout northern China, and naturally he asked Zhang Xiluan, the nominal commander-in-chief in Fengtian province, what his views were. The latter did himself a disservice by advising Yuan to 'think about it a bit more'. Zhang Zuolin, always the opportunist, enthusiastically supported Yuan's self-enthronement, probably realizing that it would not last long and could always be repudiated later. Predictably, Zhang Xiluan was transferred from Fengtian a few months after his well-intentioned counsel to Yuan Shikai. Another of Yuan's supporters, Duan Zhigui, was appointed in his place, with authority over the other two Manchurian provinces of Jilin and Heilongjiang in addition. This was a blow to Zhang Zuolin, but he played the sycophant again and made a great show of welcoming Duan Zhigui to Mukden, and he sent a telegram to Yuan in Peking confirming his loyalty. Yuan was duly enthroned on 12 December 1915. In his first honours list he named Zhang Zuolin as a marquis, second class; but when Zhang, who had no formal education to speak of, asked his entourage what that honour was worth, they told him it was rather low. Thereupon he went into a a fit of sulks — made worse by the fact that the title of his enfeoffment in Chinese, Zijue, included the word *zi* which means 'son' or 'child'. This meant, in his eyes, that Yuan Shikai regarded him as owing Yuan the filial piety of a son — a considerable slight.

Yuan's assumption of the imperial yellow alienated the revolutionaries in south and south-west China, and the Yunnan provincial commander, Cai E, rebelled. This marked in earnest the beginning of the North–South split, but Zhang Zuolin was not eager to be involved; he still had to consolidate his position in Manchuria.

In March 1916, Zhang expelled Duan Qirui's military governor from Mukden. Zhang had been abetted in his mutiny by the Japanese military commanders in the Kwantung

Army. In April the Peking government accepted the *fait accompli*, and Yuan Shikai appointed Zhang Zuolin to superintend military affairs in Fengtian. After Yuan's death in 1916, Zhang was given the titles of *dujun* and provincial civil governor in Fengtian, the essential combination of powers that constituted a major warlord.

As time passed, signs began to appear which indicated that the presence of Japanese troops — indeed any foreign troops — on Chinese soil was more and more difficult to bear. There was no stopping Japan in her grab for the resources and markets of Manchuria. Zhang's across-the-board capitulation to the Japanese demands was yet another Chinese humiliation, yet another step on the road to general war between China and Japan, though it would take another two decades to burst out in full force. The Japanese continued to watch Zhang Zuolin as a possible future ally. He was a sworn enemy of the Chinese revolution centred on Canton, and his feuds with Peking augured well for a Japanese policy of divide-and-rule in China.

Zhang Zuolin sat on the fence in Mukden during the restoration episode of 1917, but came down on the side of Duan Qirui when it was clear that Zhang Xun could not sustain his rebellion. This foolish act had brought a small windfall to Zhang Zuolin in Mukden. His subordinate Feng Tielin, who had unsuccessfully plotted against him, was implicated in the attempt to restore the Manchus, giving Zhang the excuse to imprison him and dismiss him from his command, and to absorb into his own command Feng's soldiers in the process. A further accretion to his power came in August when he took control of northernmost Heilongjiang province, on the Russian frontier, following a rebellion there which had resulted in the flight of the local *dujun*.

In October 1917, Zhang Zuolin took advantage of the fact that the *dujun* of Jilin, the third of the Manchurian provinces, had been linked to Zhang Xun's restoration bid, and got the Jilin members of the non-sitting parliament in Peking to agitate for his dismissal, which duly occurred.

Zhang's control of Manchuria was now complete, except of course for the parts held by the Japanese.

In February 1918, Duan Qirui sent his unpopular confidant, Xu Shucheng, to try and persuade Zhang to join in the Anfu Group's war with Wu Peifu and his Zhili armies (see discussion on Duan Qirui). As a bribe, Xu brought from Duan the information that a shipload of Japanese arms worth some 30,000 yuan — enough to equip seven mixed brigades — had put in at the port of Qinhuangdao. Zhang sent two of his commanders to investigate and had the arms confiscated.

In response to this friendly gesture, Zhang sent 50,000 of his troops southwards to join in Duan's campaign for 'unification of China by force'. The Peking government rewarded him with the official title of Inspector of the Three [North-eastern] Provinces. He was becoming known in China as 'king of the North-east'.

In April 1919, the growing hostility between Zhang in Mukden and the government of Premier Duan at Peking had come to a head. Zhang had never given Duan much material assistance in the latter's bid to unify China by force. And Zhang had been alienated by Duan's appointment of 'little' Xu Shucheng to command the north-western frontier provinces of Chahar and Suiyuan (roughly equivalent to modern Inner Mongolia and Ningxia) and the former imperial domains of Rehe (formerly Jehol, now Chengde).

The Northwest Army had the power to command the troops of Inner Mongolia, Xinjiang, Gansu, and Shaanxi. After Xu took up his appointment, he set up banks in the north-west, and raised a public loan, increasing his own power, which at the time was greater than that of the Inspector of the Three Provinces of Manchuria, Zhang.

This aroused Zhang Zuolin's displeasure, because he regarded Mongolia as well as Manchuria as being within his sphere of influence. So Zhang now decided to ally himself with the Zhili warlords under marshals Wu Peifu and Cao Kun, and with them fight against Xu and the rest of the Anfu Group.

In March 1920, Zhang arranged a feast in Mukden for the prominent figures of the day, inviting the representatives of the provinces of Zhili, Jiangsu, Jiangxi, Hubei, Henan, Liaoning, Jilin, and Heilongjiang. The idea was to hold a secret conference and set up an eight-province alliance, united against the Anfu Group headed by Duan Qirui.

In this intense period of confrontation between Wu Peifu's Zhili troops and those of Duan Qirui's Anfu Group, Zhang Zuolin appeared at first to play the role of mediator. Accepting an invitation to meet President Xu Shichang, a former high official under the Manchu dynasty, he rode into Peking on a train mounted with machine-guns and carrying two whole battalions of guards.

The American writer Nathaniel Peffer has left a vivid description of Zhang:

Until his triumphal entry into Peking in 1920, Chang Tso-lin [Zhang Zuolin] had not come down out of his Mukden fastness for years. In those years a legend had grown up round him — a legend of a fierce, uncouth, primitive creature of the wilds. It was with some zest, therefore, that I accepted an invitation of his nearly English-speaking secretary to attend an audience for foreign correspondents. It was with even greater amazement that I found myself bowing to a slender, delicate little person in subdued silks, soft-spoken and with hands as lovely and graceful as I have ever seen on a man. The terror of the north country looked like a precious aesthete. There was nothing of the aesthete in his speech or his demeanour, however. The interview was marked by none of the usual subtle evasion, the nice circumlocution. There was blunt talk on both sides; and it was eloquent that, when our questions verged on the brutally frank, the secretary who interpreted did not translate them as they were put, but softened them until the meaning was transformed. The quailing of the servitors when the tea was a second late also was eloquent. When he recommended the execution of a whole regi-

ment as a proper punishment for mutiny, one was glad
the regiment was not in his command.[2]

On meeting President Xu, Zhang told him that as far as he
was concerned, there was no such thing as the Zhili Group
or the Anfu Group. All should co-operate in the general
Northern cause.

None the less, Zhang travelled from Peking to Baoding to
see the Zhili group's leader Cao Kun. He also prevailed on
President Xu to dismiss the unpopular Xu Shucheng from all
his posts, much to the President's irritation. President Xu
invited Zhang to his residence when the latter returned from
Baoding, planning to have him killed over dinner. But
Premier Duan, recalling the support Zhang had given him in
the past, would not agree to the plan, and Zhang, sensing
danger, left for Manchuria.

Zhang Zuolin thereafter discarded his role of 'mediator'
and after returning to Mukden in disguise, sent a telegram to
President Xu and Premier Duan Qirui saying that in future
he would 'mediate with military force'.

Premier Duan prepared for battle, and forced President Xu
to 'dismiss' Cao Kun and Zhang Zuolin from their posts. On
10 July, Duan gave the order for a general counter-attack
against the Manchurians. Wu Peifu attacked Peking from the
south. On 12 July, Zhang and Cao challenged Duan with
telegrams, and thus the Zhili–Anfu war officially broke out,
with Zhang Zuolin supporting Zhili. On 14 July, contact was
made, and for four days both sides fought in the area of the
Liuli River. As a result, Duan's Anfu forces were badly beaten,
and he resigned all his posts. On 23–4 July, the Manchurian
and Zhili forces pursued their drive on Peking, separately
accepting the surrender of the garrison's northern and southern barracks.

In this war Zhang Zuolin had merely put a very heavy
force on the Zhili flank, and sat back without suffering any

[2] Nathaniel Peffer, 'Currents and Characters in China', *Asia*, January
1922.

damage. His and Wu Peifu's forces now occupied Peking. He had seized a large amount of military impedimenta, and it reportedly needed one hundred railway wagons to send them all up to Mukden. Twelve captured aircraft were also sent north.

The Manchurian and Zhili forces rivalled each other in rifling Anfu supplies and soon quarrelled. When the Anfu troops in Peking were being disarmed, the Manchurian officer in charge found two searchlights which had fallen into the hands of the Zhili men. Zhang Zuolin immediately asked for them, arousing the indignation of the Zhili troops. Cao Kun reportedly said: 'Zhang is really a bandit! He's got so much stuff already, and he still wants these searchlights!' Besides seizing much military equipment, Zhang Zuolin won a big increase in the size of his forces through the recruitment of soldiers of the defeated Anfu army.

When a joint Manchurian–Zhili government had been formed, on 13 August, Zhang received Japanese journalists in Tientsin and told them about his policies. He said the reason he had brought his troops south was simply that 'minor people in Duan Qirui's entourage wanted to kill me'. He promised 'mutual collaboration' with the Japanese and said that from now on he would exert his efforts to improve Japanese–Chinese relations. After this, the Japanese stepped up their support for Zhang.

Duan Qirui had resigned his premiership and sought sanctuary in the Japanese consulate at Tientsin, confirming the suspicion that he was only a poor kind of patriot. The fact was that no military leader in north China could fail to be influenced by Japan's growing military might and the Japanese interest in local rulers whom it could intimidate or buy to act as its puppets — a lesson Japan put to good use in the 1930s.

The new Peking government under Jin Yunpeng, an associate of Duan Qirui who was related to Zhang by marriage, made Zhang commissioner for Suiyuan, Chahar, and Rehe — he was now at the height of his power and influence. Still avid for national power, Zhang convened a conference of his senior commanders at Mukden in March 1922, and in the following month led his troops south into Zhili province to attack Peking, meeting Wu Peifu's troops in battle for the first time. Zhang's forces, though numerically superior, were beaten, and he retreated to Manchuria, proclaiming the independence of the three north-eastern provinces, with himself as civil and military governor. His alliance with the Zhili Group had been brief.

In September 1922, Zhang Zuolin sent a delegation to Sun Yatsen in Canton, to feel out the prospects for joint co-operation against Wu Peifu and his Zhili army. Sun sent the leftist Wang Jingwei to Mukden to discuss this idea further with Zhang. Meanwhile the latter spent one million yuan on the purchase of Japanese military equipment originally stored at Vladivostok for the invasion of Siberia, and employed Japanese engineers to build arsenals for his troops. (Vladivostok, the greatest naval port on the Russian Pacific seaboard, had been under the control of White Russian forces and the interventionist armies of the First World War allies, who sought to oppose the victory of Bolshevism. It fell to the Soviet Red Army in November 1922.)

At this point our narrative is joined by one of the most extraordinary and colourful foreigners ever to pop up in China, Frank Sutton. Sutton's biographer, Charles Drage, gives this account of his first meeting with Zhang:

> Marshal Chang Tso-lin — 'the Old Tiger' — loved to review his armies, and since he was something of a martinet, the casual onlooker would always have found his reviews sufficiently impressive, while, at this particular period, what with the general tightening of discipline and the numerous executions that had followed Chang Tso-lin's reverses of the previous spring, the standard of smartness was even higher than usual. He himself was mounted on a great dappled-grey charger with flowing mane and tail. Resplendent — if a trifle top-heavy — in full-dress uniform with heavy gold epaulets and fes-

tooned with medals, his breast studded with the stars of
orders, the whole surmounted by a gold-laced hat with
a tall, white egret-feather plume, he made a figure of
unmatchable military magnificence.

The long lines of soldiers had presented arms on his
appearance and now stood motionless, rifles at the 'slope'
and swords at the 'carry', while, followed by a glittering
bevy of aides-de-camp and equerries, he rode slowly down
the ranks. Suddenly a mighty hubbub arose behind him
and he wheeled his horse to see an astonishing spectacle.
An ancient Model-T Ford had forced its way through the
crowds of onlookers and was heading straight towards
him. It was driven by a gigantic European, and on the seat
beside him shone the polished barrel of a small cannon.
Police and staff officers converged from all sides, drawing
their revolvers as they ran. The car was soon brought to a
standstill and surrounded; but, instead of meekly allowing
himself to be escorted off the parade ground, the big man
stood upright on the driver's seat and could be seen above
the heads of the indignant officials gesticulating wildly
and brandishing the stump of an arm and bellowing like
a bull.[3]

The importunate giant was an Englishman, Frank Sutton,
who had lost an arm while fighting the Turks at Gallipoli in
the First World War, but gone on to be a prospector in
Siberia. He had offered his services as military adviser and
engineer to both Sun Yatsen and Wu Peifu, and been
rebuffed by them, finally fetching up at Mukden to try his
luck with Zhang Zuolin.

Zhang had at first refused to see Sutton, and the latter's
electrifying appearance at the military review was his way of
cutting through the bureaucratic underbrush to get to the
'Old Tiger'.

Rather than having Sutton shot on the spot, Marshal
Zhang demanded an instant demonstration, and got one.
The 'small cannon' turned out to be a field-mortar designed

[3] Charles Drage, *Soldier of Fortune*, London: Heinemann, 1963, p. 163.

and built by Sutton himself, though he had only five rounds. The demonstration impressed the Manchurian warlord so much that he gave Sutton three weeks to make more ammunition and give another performance. This also went well, the barrel of the mortar becoming too hot to hold after it had been fired at targets between 200 and 2,000 yards away. Undaunted, Sutton added a finale by picking up the mortar with his good arm, running forward with it, and setting it up to fire again.

Duly impressed, Zhang appointed him Master General of Ordnance to the Manchurian armies with a down-payment of 15,000 pounds sterling. His first job was to re-equip the Mukden arsenal, which was of noted inefficiency and subject to corruption among the officials who ran it. Thus began Sutton's three-year-long association with Zhang Zuolin.

The Mukden arsenal was in a shocking state. Imported machinery lay rusting. Money had been wasted trying to produce aircraft. The poison-gas factory, mercifully, had not even been equipped. But there were plenty of raw materials and Sutton got to work. By mid-1924 the arsenal was producing good-quality rifles and machine-guns, hand-grenades, and 200,000 rounds of ammunition every day. He designed his own artillery and made his own field telephones.

This engineering genius trod a tightrope with the 'Old Marshal' (Zhang Zuolin), who was sometimes exasperated by his blunt stubbornness over technical matters, but Sutton hit it off well with his son, Xueliang, who was soon to be a famous commander. He also pursued his favourite sports of one-arm golf and rugby football, playing with British members of the Mukden Club.

In September 1923, when the old warlord Cao Kun bribed members of the Peking parliament to vote him in as president, Zhang, his recent ally, protested against this in an open telegram. Zhang and other prominent leaders had withdrawn their representatives from the venal, do-nothing body, and Cao grabbed the presidency easily by forcing the incumbent, Li Yuanhong, to sign his own resignation. Members of what was popularly called the 'pig parliament' had received 5,000 yuan each for Cao Kun's election.

In 1924, Cao Kun and Wu Peifu reached agreement with the Christian General Feng Yuxiang to mount an expedition against Manchuria and bring down the arrogant Zhang Zuolin once and for all. In September Wu's troops marched north to stage the initial battle at Shanhaiguan. Feng pretended to follow, but at the last moment he turned back and occupied Peking, controlling the railways, posts, and all other forms of communication between the capital and the rest of the country. Wu was caught between Feng's troops and the Manchurians and fled to north China by ship. Feng deposed 'President' Cao Kun, and between them he and Zhang Zuolin persuaded Duan Qirui to come out of retirement once more and take the title of 'provisional chief executive'.

Duan may not have been the world's most effective administrator, but he had experience at the top and there were precious few people around with his detachment and philosophical approach. None the less his tenure this time lasted only until April 1926, when he was again deposed and resumed his retirement to study Buddhism and play mahjong. Zhang, hard put to it to find a competent head of government, took the post himself in mid-1927 and held it until 1928.

Meanwhile Zhang was being brought face-to-face with the economic realities of warlordism. It ruined crops, massacred workers and peasants, debased the currency, and interfered with the maintenance of roads and railways. Living principally on various kinds of tax and excise — or plain foraging and looting — the warlords systematically destroyed their own sources of income to buy arms and (occasionally) pay their troops. They squandered the country's wealth on their own luxuriating life-style, and borrowed money recklessly at home and abroad.

Not the least of China's economic problems in the 1920s was the bewildering variety of paper currencies issued by different cities and provinces — for instance Shandong, Harbin, Tientsin, and Hankou. The Japanese demanded the use of yen in Dalian and along the South Manchurian Railway, according to Hallett Abend, the correspondent of the *New York Times*. Staff at hotels and rickshaw drivers would scornfully reject tips paid in small silver coins minted in the next province, since it was impossible to tell at a glance how debased the coinage was. The one stable medium of exchange was the silver dollar based originally on the silver content of the Mexican dollar, which circulated in most parts of the country.

By no means the most stupid of the warlords, Zhang Zuolin had become committed by the mid-1920s to a paper currency whose backing went from bad to worse. Between 1917 and 1927, a silver dollar's value in Manchurian paper currency units went from 1.27 to 10.61, which even in the modern world would be reckoned a pretty severe inflation.[4]

There was also the problem of disaffection, a thorn-in-the-side of any warlord. Despite their high-sounding pledges of loyalty to their superiors, teachers, and classmates, the warlords throve on treachery and trusted each other as little as they trusted the revolutionaries in the south. Their friends often turned into their worst enemies. In November 1925, General Guo Songling, one of Zhang's top commanders, turned against him and signed a secret 'peace treaty' with Feng Yuxiang, who at that particular moment was warring with Zhang (one could never tell which side Feng would land up on in any fight).

Guo and Feng, in their secret pact, agreed to eradicate warlordism and overthrow Zhang Zuolin. This was surely a case of the 'pot calling the kettle black', but the warlords loved to quote humanitarian motives when they intrigued with one

---

[4] Ch'i Hsi-sheng, *Warlord Politics in China 1916–1928*, Stanford: Stanford University Press, 1976, p. 163.

another. General Guo, who was campaigning in Zhili (Hebei) at the time, was suddenly summoned back to Mukden by Zhang. Not surprisingly he was worried by the invitation, and decided to show his hand straight away. He took the surprising step of arranging a meeting with Zhang's son, Xueliang, to propose that if his father were deposed, Xueliang should succeed him. Then he telegraphed Zhang Zuolin in Mukden to the effect that he was on his way in obedience to the order.

Going only as far as Luanzhou, in Zhili, Guo hurriedly convened a military conference with his subordinates and announced that he was changing sides. More than thirty of his senior officers refused to support him, so he locked them up. He then sent out an open telegram, listing the evils of Zhang's rule in Manchuria. Guo's men occupied Shanhaiguan, on the strategic coastal road to Manchuria. Shanhaiguan is the point where the Great Wall — almost literally — touches the sea. On 27 November, Zhang sent his son to Shanhaiguan to negotiate a ceasefire with Guo. Guo refused to receive him, but later sent Xueliang a long letter detailing his grievances against his father.

Zhang Zuolin offered a reward of 800,000 yuan for Guo's head, but at the same time invited reconciliation when he dismissed another of his commanders whom Guo, apparently, had particularly hated. On 6 December Zhang was sufficiently alarmed by Guo's advance that he astonishingly announced his resignation and prepared to take refuge in Japanese-controlled Dalian. At the same time he invited the Japanese Kwantung Army commander, General Hirogawa, to come to Mukden and signed a secret agreement with him.

The Japanese command then issued an order forbidding military activity within ten miles of the South Manchurian Railway, which they controlled and garrisoned. This made it difficult for Guo to continue his advance on Mukden. Two senior Japanese officers went to see Guo, and delivered a warning to him in person, which the Chinese general rejected. On 9 December the Japanese set up a field headquarters

at Mukden, and in Tokyo the cabinet decided to send reinforcements. A 3,000-man brigade from Guo's army penetrated as far as Yingkou, but was stopped by the Japanese. A decisive battle began, involving the Japanese, Guo's troops, and
Zhang's Manchurian army. Guo was defeated, and he and his
wife were captured and summarily shot on Zhang Zuolin's
personal instructions. The intervention of Japanese soldiers
in an internal Chinese problem was seized on by the Chinese
communists and others as a political cause. Manchurian students in Japan joined in the protests, denouncing Zhang for
his collaboration with the Japanese.

The next round of the military-political minuet among the
warlords occurred in early 1926, when Zhang Zuolin
telegraphed to Wu Peifu, who was operating in central China
at the time, proposing that they co-operate to resist the
Christian General Feng Yuxiang. The Southern revolutionaries in Canton were preparing for their Northern
Expedition, and there were grounds to fear that the mercurial Feng would join their cause. The bulk of Feng's forces at
that time were in defensive positions in the mountains
around Nankou, near Peking, while Feng himself was preparing to go to Moscow to seek Soviet aid. The need to keep up
pressure on the 'Christian' troops at Nankou was to prove a
major impediment to Wu Peifu in his attempts to resist the
advance of the Northern Expedition forces from the south
towards Wuhan, on the Yangtze.

Tokyo, meanwhile, was at its usual game of 'muddying the
waters to catch fish'. In March 1926, the Manchurian and
Shandong armies attacked Feng's troops at the Tagu forts
guarding the approaches to Tientsin, which had figured so
prominently in the seafaring powers' attacks on China in the
nineteenth century. Japanese ships had been using the port
to supply the Manchurian and Shandong forces with arms,
but this time Feng Yuxiang got wind of what was happening
and succeeded in having the port sealed off, on the grounds
that foreign warships must fly their flags and submit to
inspection when entering. The Japanese forced the port with

two destroyers to cover the unloading of arms for the Manchurians. There was an exchange of fire between the destroyers and the port batteries, which Tokyo made into a diplomatic incident. An anti-Japanese demonstration of students in Peking was put down with the loss of forty-six lives on 1 March — somewhat exaggeratedly described by the author Lu Xun as 'the blackest day in Chinese history'.

The Manchurians with their Shandong allies and the Zhili forces under Wu Peifu took advantage of Feng's preoccupation with this incident to attack his troops in northern Zhili, forcing the Christians to fall back towards Peking. On 23 March the Manchurians occupied Tientsin.

The spring and early summer of 1926 saw more riots and demonstrations by students in Peking, which as usual were suppressed by force. Zhang Zuolin meanwile conferred with Marshal Wu Peifu, and they agreed to attack the Southern revolutionary army, which was then preparing its Northern Expedition. But they wasted much time in talk, while the Southerners began to roll through the country at an astonishing speed.

By October they had chased Wu Peifu up the Peking–Hankou railway and were simultaneously advancing through Jiangxi. On 14 October, with the situation becoming increasingly menacing for the warlords, Zhang Zuolin convened a conference in Tientsin, attended by representatives of Wu Peifu, by the tyrannical Zhang Zongchang of Shandong in person, and by other senior commanders of the various regional groupings. However Yan Xishan of Shanxi province did not attend, and this, coupled with Wu Peifu's absence, made Zhang wary of adopting any too sweeping schemes.

In a surprise move, the Shandong-born Nanking warlord, Sun Chuanfang, suddenly turned up, asking for aid and offering his loyalty, to the delight of the other Northerners. With east China in disarray, it was Sun's only chance of survival as a big warlord, and he expressed his wish to retire to Zhejiang province while the Shandong armies of Zhang

Zongchang would be invited to occupy Jiangsu, and the Manchurians would be begged to hold a line on the left (north) bank of the Yangtze.

This development put Zhang Zuolin at the head of the largest joint military force in north China, but there were grave doubts about its inner unity. Each warlord was basically in search of greater power and wealth for himself, and none of them trusted the other. For fear of offending the absent Wu and Yan, Zhang declined to take high-sounding titles such as commander-in-chief, and despite Sun Chuanfang's unexpected offer of alliance, the Tientsin conference achieved little.

By late 1926, China was split along the Yangtze, with the KMT forces poised to attack directly towards Peking along the railway northwards from Wuhan, and through Jiangxi province into the lower Yangtze region. But politically the KMT was split between the leftists and Communists at Wuhan and the pro-Chiang Kaishek forces at Nanking. A mass breakdown of the revolutionary effort could be envisaged soon, if Chiang could not pull his armies together and establish his authority over the Soviet-backed wing of the KMT at Wuhan.

In late November, the Shandong and east China warlords persuaded Zhang Zuolin to accept the title of 'Commander-in-Chief of the National Pacification Army' (*Anguojun*) — adding yet another high-sounding title to the shambling masses of soldiery who tramped back and forth across China. Zhang proclaimed the only political stand his disparate allies had in common: anti-Communism.

Both the British and the Japanese had a keen interest in the events in China. The new British minister to China, Miles Lampson, was instructed by the Foreign Office to visit the left-KMT leadership at Wuhan where he held discussions with Eugene Chen, the KMT Foreign Minister. Later he also visited Zhang Zuolin to feel out the possibilities for peace. (As a precaution, the British were getting ready a full division of troops to protect their nationals and interests in the Yangzi basin.)

The Japanese, on the other hand, were anxious that Chiang Kaishek should concentrate his attention on destroying the Communists. Perhaps the often-prescient Japanese saw that, in the long run, the Communists were a greater threat to their aim of dominating all of China than was the KMT. They urged both Chiang and Zhang Zuolin to pursue a policy of harmony among Northern and Southern factions in order better to deal with the Communists.

Playing on the differences among the warlords, Chiang Kaishek held secret discussions with Zhang Zuolin's envoys in March 1927, regarding the possibility of Zhang using his Manchurian troops to destroy the left-wingers and Communists at Wuhan — an extraordinary act of cynicism on Chiang Kaishek's part. Zhang, however, decided to do a little 'red-hunting' (*taochi*) on his own. He had the Soviet embassy in Peking raided and its files ransacked. Inside were hiding thirty-six KMT members, including the veteran revolutionary and Marxist theorist, Li Dazhao. Li and others were condemned to death and strangled on a gibbet which is now in the Museum of the History of the Revolution.

In late March and early April, the final stages of the first part of the Northern Expedition were accomplished. Kuomintang forces surged down the Yangzi and took first Nanking and then Shanghai. In Shanghai, Chiang Kaishek's commanders perpetrated a fearful massacre of Communist trade union leaders, workers, students, and anybody who got in the way. From 12–14 April KMT commanders in other places — Canton, Guangxi, and the big east China ports — took their cue from Shanghai and put down the local Communists in a sea of blood. Only in their stronghold of Wuhan did the Communists escape, and they had to face the fact that they were now alone — most of southern China being firmly in the hands of Chiang Kaishek and his allies. Chiang took this opportunity to declare the formation of a KMT government at Nanking, thus increasing Wuhan's isolation.

Zhang Zuolin, encouraged by the consolidation of his power and by feelers from Chiang Kaishek, decided to test his strength against the pro-Communist armies. In early May, the Manchurians and their east-China allies, Zhang Zongchang and Sun Chuanfang, attacked on two fronts. As Zhang Zuolin's men pushed down the Peking–Hankou railway, Zhang Zongchang and Sun came south via Xuzhou, to reach the Yangzi at Pukou, near Nanking.

In face of the common threat, Wuhan and KMT-controlled Nanking put their differences aside for a while and agreed to continue the Northern Expedition, even if it meant a head-on clash with the Manchurians. The forces of Nanking and Wuhan jointly assaulted the Manchurians and pushed them back with victory after victory. The Eastern warlords were driven back to Xuzhou, with their backs to Shandong as their only sanctuary from the KMT assault.

Meanwhile the Christians commanded by Feng Yuxiang were pushing down the Yellow River by way of the ancient city of Loyang to take the medieval capital (of the Northern Song dynasty) of Kaifeng. So China's ancient civil wars were fought again. Wuhan and Nanking were now in competition with each other for Feng's favours and the assistance of his Russian-equipped army. Nanking prevailed in June.

Chiang Kaishek, in addition to winning the support of Feng Yuxiang, had put out feelers to Zhang Zuolin for a peaceful settlement. He proposed that Zhang's force drop its title of National Pacification Army and be integrated into the KMT's National Revolutionary Army. Marshal Zhang should then announce his subscription to the Three People's Principles of Dr Sun Yatsen and be entrusted with guarding the security of Manchuria.

Zhang Zuolin was not impressed, and instead proclaimed himself Commander-in-Chief of the Chinese Republican Land Armies, and Prime Minister of the National Pacification Army Government. Then he sent out a circular telegram, calling again for negotiations with Chiang Kaishek to 'oppose the Reds', and implausibly describing himself as an 'old friend' of Sun Yatsen.

Chiang's permanently strained relations with the Japanese

were now again under a shadow. The Tokyo Foreign Ministry had recommended that Japan drop its support for him. This went hand-in-hand with the Japanese Government's decision to reinforce its troops in Shandong, which it considered its rightful sphere of influence, and which Chiang Kaishek was poised to invade — indeed KMT troops were already present on Shandong's southern coast.

The Japanese Kwantung Army commander sent a seaborne expedition of 2,000 men to the port of Qingdao, and throughout June continued the build-up with seasoned troops. The Japanese commanding general took it upon himself to send toops up the railway line from Qingdao to Jinan, the provincial capital of Shandong. On 2 May, Chiang Kaishek asked the Japanese commander to withdraw from the positions his men had taken up to guard the Japanese settlements in Jinan and along the railway. Fighting broke out between the Japanese and KMT soldiers, and Tokyo dispatched further reinforcements to the accompaniment of its habitual list of humiliating demands for apologies and restitution. The Japanese attacked and overwhelmed the Chinese forces, with thousands of Chinese casualties. The chances of peace between China and Japan were more remote than ever now, and the Japanese had tightened their grip on Shandong, unchallenged by the oppressive Zhang Zongchang, whose army was on the brink of collapse.

Throughout May 1928, Zhang Zuolin in Peking flirted on one side with Chiang Kaishek and on the other with the Japanese who warned him that he had better return to Mukden because of the deteriorating situation. Japan then issued a warning to Chiang Kaishek and Feng Yuxiang to the effect that, should war break out in north-east China, Japan would have to 'take measures to maintain order'. Zhang Zuolin decided to withdraw his forces to Manchuria. He issued orders to the effect that his seal, and the banner of 'Grand Marshal of the National Pacification Army', as well as important files at the Foreign Ministry and the State Council, be shipped to Mukden.

As the Northern Expedition forces approached Peking,

Zhang took leave of the diplomatic corps and assigned the security of Peking to the police force and a single Manchurian brigade. He announced for the benefit of the people of China that he was retiring to Manchuria because of his failure to exterminate the Communists. On the evening of 2 June, in a bright yellow limousine, he drove out of the Zhongnanhai park-like residential area attached to the Forbidden City. On his arrival at Peking railway station (which was then about a mile to the west of its present location), he was seen off by an honour guard and boarded the sky-blue armoured coach, luxuriously decorated inside, which used to be reserved for the Empress Dowager Cixi.

In the early hours of 4 June, when it was barely light, Zhang's train passed under a bridge at the junction of the Mukden–Peking railway and the South Manchurian railway controlled by the Japanese. There was a massive explosion, the bridge collapsed, and Zhang was pulled from the wreckage, fatally injured. His aides commandeered a passing wedding car — expelling the bride — to rush Zhang to his residence in Mukden. He died in the car, but the top officials of his Manchurian government decided to hush up his death until his son, Xueliang, could return from Tientsin where he was supervising arrangements for the evacuation of the Manchurian troops there. Food was cooked and medicine brought in, ostensibly for the Old Marshal, who was said to be only lightly injured. Xueliang disguised himself as a woman and hurried back to Mukden.

The Japanese, who had hoped to see Manchuria descend into chaos with the death of Zhang, and to profit from it, had mined the railway line with thirty bags of gunpowder which were detonated by remote control. Though they doubtless suspected that Zhang was dead because of the sheer force of the explosion, they could not say so for fear of compromising themselves. Japan still had to take at least marginal account of world opinion and was already feeling British and American pressure to stop interfering in Manchurian affairs. Zhang Xueliang duly inherited his father's position as overlord of Manchuria.

Wu Peifu[5]

Wu Peifu was the most respected of all the warlords — with the possible exception of Feng Yuxiang. He was the best military commander, and one of the few who by Chinese standards were not considered corrupt. His tragedy was to be thrust by circumstances into meaningless wars in which he was betrayed by his allies. Wu professed indifference to politics, but his stand on some important political issues proved to be crucial, and intentionally or not he did as much as anyone to bring about the downfall of the warlords as a ruling class.

Born into a poor gentry family in Shandong province, with no particular wealth or influence to back him up, Wu succeeded in taking the degree of *xiucai* ('budding talent'), which bespoke a good grasp of the Chinese classical works of literature and philosophy. Had he pursued the profession of letters, he might have risen high in the imperial civil service. But after taking this degree in 1896, he decided on a military career and in due course was enrolled at the Baoding military academy. There he graduated in 1903 and received a commission in the Imperial Third Division commanded by General Cao Kun. He caught Cao's eye as a promising young officer and the two were closely associated for most of their active lives — a student–teacher relationship which did much to shape the destinies of post-revolutionary China.

When the Revolution broke out in 1911, Cao and Wu were sent to suppress its manifestations in the northern province of Shanxi. Both were conservatives by inclination and training, and doubtless felt moderately at ease under the dictatorial rule established by Yuan Shikai on the overthrow of the Manchus. In 1917, as a brigadier, Wu was involved in the suppression of Zhang Xun's attempt to restore the Manchu

[5] The authoritative biography of Wu Peifu in English is by Odoric Wou, *Militarism in Modern China: The Career of Wu P'ei-fu*, New York: Columbia University Press, 1978.

dynasty, and then was dispatched to fight the Southern revolutionaries in Hunan province. The fighting in Hunan did
not go well for long for the Northerners and progress was
very slow, although they did occupy the provincial capital of
Changsha. The troops became demoralized by the rain,
flooding, food shortages, and epidemics.

In Peking the ruling circles were locked in intrigue, largely
concerning the question of whether the premier or the president should act as commander-in-chief of the army. Wu
Peifu was incensed at all the intriguing behind his back while
he was trying to score a total military victory in Hunan and
destroy the Southern revolutionary forces. In August 1918,
when the Hunan war had been fought to a standstill, Wu
raised his voice in protest against further pursuance of the
fratricide. He sent out an open telegram in his somewhat
flowery, literary Chinese, saying that Premier Duan's policy
of reunifying China by force was a course of ruin for the
country. The Peking government was 'erroneously listening
to the voices of traitors', and was 'involved in self-serving
hostilities and alliances, regarding south-west China as an
enemy, and considering peace-talks to represent a rebellious
counter-current'.

Wu acknowledged that it was the duty of military men to
follow orders, but argued that to resist policies ruinous to
China could not be seen as mere disobedience, but rather as
a diagnosis of the country's condition. He said the National
Assembly convened in place of the 1912 parliament was 'useless as a wart'. He also denounced Premier Duan's policy of
relying on Japanese support. 'The Japanese', he fulminated,
'want to take advantage of our distress to mobilize their
troops, and an agreement that will humiliate China has
already been drawn up. ... The civil war has gone on for over
a year. Chinese are borrowing money to kill other Chinese,
as though slaking their thirst with poisoned wine.'

Wu's denunciations were a serious blow to Duan's prestige.
Although some *dujuns* had called for an end to the civil war,
not even the revolutionaries in the south and south-west

had used such strong language to him. Furthermore, Wu's change of position had taken place over quite a short period of time: only three months previously he had been the strongest advocate and firmest implementer of the policy of reunification by force. He had even written a poem about his capture of the southern Hunan city of Hengyang. What Duan and his cabinet did not know was that Wu had reached a secret understanding with the Guangxi Group in the south-west to hasten the advent of peace.

Other *dujuns* also found Wu's attitude impertinent. He was, after all, no more than a division commander. And his outspokenness had become an embarrassment to his old mentor and patron, Cao Kun, who as governor of Zhili made his headquarters at the provincial capital of Baoding, although he also spent part of his time in Tientsin. Wu sent him a conciliatory message, saying he would come north and make amends for his insubordination as soon as an amnesty and peace talks between north and south were declared. The Guangxi leaders applauded Wu's statements (not the most helpful thing for him in the circumstances), and said that his latest telegram 'like a thunderclap, has split the dark clouds'.

Wu had a formidable reputation as a commander, despite his failure to conquer Hunan completely, and nobody was anxious to take him on in battle. Various *dujuns* came out with denunciations of Wu Peifu. The governor of Anhui — the only pro-Duan commander in the Yangzi basin — accused Wu of 'quibbling about law while the overall situation goes from bad to worse'. Another denounced him for 'wily words which distort the facts, for egotism and selfishness'. He was portrayed as having already concluded an alliance with the south-west, which was not far from the truth. But no one dared attack him.

The stalemate continued for over a year, with Wu sitting it out in Hengyang, constantly demanding to be transferred north. The Peking government stopped paying him his men's wages for the last eight months.

Wu's code of ethics was strangely flexible at times. From 1919 on he began a flirtation with, of all people, the Chinese Communists, who were not even officially incorporated as a party until 1921, but were active in the left wing of the Kuomintang. They influenced various representative bodies, for instance the so-called National Federation of All Circles of the People, which had its headquarters in Shanghai. Originally the Communists, in accordance with their Leninist dogma, regarded Wu as an opportunist who won cheap popularity by his anti-war, anti-Japanese stand. Nor did the Kuomintang like Wu's cordiality with the Guangxi leaders, whom it wanted to dominate. None the less, Wu Peifu's popularity could not be disregarded. His military power lent weight to his sometimes liberal pronouncements. He even fancied himself as a champion of the oppressed workers of China. (The Communists, however, had cause to regret their trust in Wu's support in 1923, when he bloodily put down a strike by workers on the Peking–Hankou Railway.)

Wu became increasingly disillusioned with his role as commander of the Northern force in the Hunan war. His troops were on paper superior to the Hunanese and not many units from the other southern provinces had gone to the latter's aid. But the campaign was metaphorically and literally bogged down in 1918, and on top of that Wu could not get enough funds from Peking to pay his troops. He was chronically short of munitions and supplies, despite the fact that he had the Peking–Hankou Railway at his back, which should have eased all physical problems of supply. To add insult to injury, Peking had appointed the incompetent, cruel, and corrupt Zhang Jingyao to be *dujun* of Hunan — a prize Wu might most reasonably have expected for himself.

Wu was also indignant at the Duan government's secret dealings with the Japanese, which he regarded as treasonable. He infuriated Peking by demanding the reconvention of the 1912 parliament and the restoration of the Provisional Constitution which Yuan Shikai had amended to increase his own power. A snowstorm of telegrams whirled across China — many of them published in the newspapers — by which means the warlords and government leaders attacked or flattered each other, in classical Chinese prose. (Many of them employed Confucian scholars for just this purpose, but the xiucai Wu, of course, could write his own.)

In August 1918, exasperated beyond measure, Wu Peifu concluded a personal ceasefire agreement with the Hunan commanders, and sent out an open telegram condemning the war and bitterly denouncing Premier Duan's policy of unifying the country by force. Commanders associated with the Zhili Group around Marshal Cao Kun expressed their agreement with Wu, and some of the pro-Anfu *dujuns* were also weary of the inconclusive mess in Hunan.

Naturally the Southern and south-western leaders welcomed Wu's initiative. After they paid him 60,000 yuan to defray his costs, he led his troops out of Hunan and — doubtless to his satisfaction the people of Changsha, the provincial capital, rose against the obnoxious Zhang Jingyao and drove him out ignominiously.

Wu Peifu then stationed his army — essentially the famous Third Division — around Luoyang, on the middle reaches of the Yellow River. An ancient capital of China, with fabulous Buddha figures carved out of naked rock along the river bank, Luoyang was relatively easy to defend; and the down-river city of Zhengzhou, capital of Henan province, made a good headquarters for any fighting in central China.

Wu had relied on his personal prestige and the reputation of the Third Division to defy the Anfu leadership politically, and he was regarded by the public as a man of honour and in some ways a progressive. This did not mean he was kindly: he did not hesitate to punish insubordination severely, or to shoot down demonstrators or strikers. He was an austere, sombre man, tall but fine-boned, with brilliant amber eyes — highly unusual in a Chinese and remembered by everyone who met him. He was extremely critical of the political situation in China, but he was a democrat only insofar as other

people's views coincided with his own. He believed warlordism should be abolished and the country's troops be
commanded by a centralized war ministry — which doubtless he would have expected to rule.

Though his heavy drinking probably masked some self-
doubt, General Wu was an extremely stubborn man who
once set on a course of action usually followed it through to
the end. But his temperament was not well suited to the
Machiavellian political atmosphere of the day. In some
respects his character was similar to that of the British
General Gordon, who had helped the Chinese imperial army
put down the Taiping Rebellion in the 1860s. The American
writer Nathaniel Peffer has left this description of Wu:

> He received me in cotton gown in a rough office with
> ordinary wooden chairs, a cheap wooden table and
> bare, unplastered walls, and privates came and went
> without ceremony. Between his quarters and those of
> his lieutenants there was no mark of distinction.
> Between his clothes and those of a moderately success-
> ful lantern-shop proprietor the distinction would be all
> in the shopkeeper's favour. Tall, thin and somewhat
> bowed, with the face and manner of a student, he, like
> Chang Tso-lin [Zhang Zuolin], looks more the esthete
> than the warrior. But unlike Chang Tso-lin, he really is
> a scholar, if not an esthete.[6]

A man like this was certain to clash with the low type of
politician to be found in Peking at the time, and while he
was favourable to certain aspects of the democratic revolution demanded by the politicians of the south, he could turn
on those who sought his help for reasons best known to
himself. Seen at one time as a potential ally of even the
Chinese Communists, he was at heart an autocrat.

Wu had his Confucian principles and his deep sense of
personal honour. He was a patriot of note, and both Britain
and the United States saw him as a force for good and a

---

[6] Peffer, 'Currents and Characters in China'.

potential protector of their interests, especially in the Yangtze valley and eastern China. In 1919, though, the Western powers were licking their wounds from the war in Europe, and were in no mood to match Japan's attempts at interference and subversion in China. They had made their own land-grabs long since.

While Wu nursed his pride in Luoyang, the never-ending round of job-swapping and musical chairs continued in Peking. President Feng Guochang, a supporter of the Zhili Group whose hands were tied by his high office, had died. The old, pro-Japanese bureaucrat, Xu Shichang, had taken his place. Now Peking was an Anfu island in the Zhili sea, whose marker-buoys were Baoding and Tientsin. At last Duan Qirui made up his mind militarily to attack Zhili positions on three different fronts, with the unpopular 'Little Xu' (Xu Shucheng) as his chief-of-staff. They styled their troops the 'National Pacification Army'. The Zhili commanders matched his mobilization, bringing their forces north from Henan and Hubei and grandly styling them the 'Destroy-the-Rebels Army'. Wu Peifu was the main field commander.

On the evening of 14 July 1920, contact was made. An Anfu unit moving out from Peking clashed with the advancing Zhili troops, which fell back on the railway town of Gaobaidian, some fifty miles south-west of the capital.

In the intense heat of the north China summer, the Anfu troops clashed with more Zhili units near Yangcun, which also fell back. For three days the armies swayed back and forth, with the Zhili troops being unexpectedly drubbed.

But the veteran Wu was not to be so easily trounced. He made a swift move from Gaopaidian and deeply penetrated the Anfu right flank, cutting the 'border defence' forces off from their rear. Their commander was taken prisoner and the rank and file panicked. The Anfu order of battle crumbled as senior officers surrendered to Wu's men and their troops threw down their weapons and ran. The collapse of the presidential bodyguard, the Fifteenth Division, led to general rout. It was the victory of professionalism and battle-hardening over badly trained, inexperienced troops. The Anfu Group was paying dearly for its insistence on keeping Wu in the field for so long in Hunan.

Now Zhang Zuolin played his hand. He announced that his Manchurians would support the Zhili forces. 'Little Xu' fled his field headquarters at Langfang, on the Peking–Tientsin Railway, and the 'border defence' troops there surrendered. On 19 July Duan Qirui announced his resignation as premier. For a moment it seemed as though the Anfu Group itself would disappear entirely from the scene. Zhili and Manchurian troops entered Peking (the Manchurians having barely fired a shot, but anxious to join in the victory). The British and Americans in Shanghai, Peking, and elsewhere were pleased rather than otherwise. The Japanese gave diplomatic protection to the Anfu leaders in their legation, and began casting their eyes on Zhang Zuolin as the man of the future in north China.

The joint occupation of Peking by the Zhili and Manchurian troops inevitably led to frictions. Zhili gained only Shaanxi province from the territorial adjustments of the victory: but Chang had won a huge windfall in the shape of Inner Mongolia, Suiyuan, Rehe, and Chahar — territory which before the war had been under the command of 'Little Xu'.

Wu might well feel aggrieved over the meagre share of the spoils he received after the defeat of the Anfu Group. But he began building his forces up in lieu of territorial gain, and this alarmed his patron and superior, Cao Kun. Wu was still dominant in Hubei province and had developed alliances with Shaanxi and Sichuan. To complicate matters, Zhang Zuolin, the Manchurian warlord, snubbed Wu as a mere division commander, and would talk only with Cao Kun. The makings of a first-rate split in the Zhili Group were present. Cao attempted to assuage General Wu's sense of grievance by making him Inspection Commissioner of Zhili, Shandong, and Henan, a post which could carry great power if the incumbent knew how to use it. But Wu lacked political flair.

In April 1922, Zhang decided to go for a military solution and moved his troops from Mukden towards Shanhaiguan on the shore of the Bohai Gulf in order to attack Peking. Wu's forces moved up and met him, with the aid of troops supplied by Feng Yuxiang, the Christian general, to whom Wu had appealed for aid. Zhang was soundly beaten and retreated north of the Great Wall again. There he began a thorough programme of training and upgrading the armament of his men, in preparation for the inevitable second war between Manchuria and Zhili.

Wu was not entirely at ease in his relations with his new ally, Feng Yuxiang. Feng's troops were mostly Henanese, but Henan was General Wu's favourite base territory and there was no room for two suns in the sky. Feng was mercurial, indeed undependable, but his men were battle-hardened and disciplined, with exceptionally high morale.

Enlightened opinion in China — such as that of the rationalist and man of letters, Hu Shi — was increasingly looking to Wu to use his new-found influence in shaping a decent national government, perhaps with elements of federalism. One reason for Wu's popularity was his consistent hostility towards the Japanese. In 1922 a conference was held in Washington between the great Western maritime powers, Japan and China. One result of this was the success of pressure put on Japan by the Western powers to remove her troops from Shandong, which she reluctantly did in 1923. Zhang Zuolin, the only Northern commander who could match Wu's effective strength, had an on-again, off-again relationship with Tokyo and was unwilling to chance his arm in a military contest with the Japanese. That left only Wu with the will and the ability to challenge them, but fortunately the Washington conference[7] rendered that unnecessary.

[7] The Washington Conference of 1922 was convened by President Harding in an effort to maintain China's territorial integrity, and to limit the growth of Japanese power in East Asia. One result was that the parts of Shandong seized by Japan from Germany at the beginning of the First World War were finally returned to China.

The Zhili alliance was now split pretty clearly between Wu's supporters in Luoyang, and Cao's group in Baoding and Tientsin. Even Dr Sun Yatsen and his Soviet advisers thought Wu a sufficiently promising ally for their envoys to discuss with him the possibility of a joint effort to eliminate warlordism and build a genuine republic. However, Dr Sun was having problems with the Guangdong *dujun* Chen Jiongming, who had rebelled against him, and the Kuomintang army was not yet ready for its Northern Expedition. Nothing came of the Sun–Wu contacts; Sun was also approached by Zhang Zuolin with a view to discussing an alliance, but the two men had little in common and that idea, too, withered on the branch.

By now Wu was arguably the most powerful man in China. More and more of the *dujuns* turned their eyes to him in the absence of any strong government in Peking, and Luoyang became for a while a kind of mini-capital for the northern part of the country. Wu now controlled, directly or indirectly, the middle and lower reaches of the Yellow River and the Yangtze, and his political influence extended as far as Fujian on the south-east coast, and even into Guangdong, where the Chen Jiongming had led a temporarily successful revolt against Sun Yatsen. He still enjoyed good will among the leaders of Guangxi, in the south-west. Had he been a better politician, he could surely have rallied the Northerners and defeated the Kuomintang with a two-pronged attack through Hunan and Fujian into Guangdong. China's subsequent history might have been very much different from the way it turned out.

In August 1924, the *dujuns* of Jiangsu and Zhejiang had begun fighting over the question of who should control Shanghai (the Chinese city and the suburbs — not, of course, the International Settlement). Manchuria backed Zhejiang and simultaneously declared war on Zhili.

Wu's Third Division moved on Shanhaiguan, Manchuria's gateway into Zhili. Zhang attempted a flanking move but Wu typically anticipated this and checked the Manchurian

1. Sun Yatsen, the 'father of the Chinese Republic'.

2. Yuan Shikai (1859-1916), the 'father' of the warlord system.

3. Yuan Shikai while provisional president of the Republic of China (1912).

4. Yuan Shikai attempted to assume the title of 'emperor'. He is shown here in a ritual of homage at the Temple of Heaven.

5. General Cai E (1859-1916), the *dujun* of Yunnan, and first provincial leader openly to declare independence in opposition to the presidency of Yuan Shikai.

6. Li Yuanhong, upon his inauguration as president of the Republic in June, 1916.

7. The Peking warlord, Duan Qirui, who became premier of the Republic in 1916.

8. Zhang Xun (1854-1923), the 'Pigtailed General', was governor of Anhui. He led a briefly successful move in 1917 to restore the last Qing dynasty emperor, Pu Yi, to the throne.

9. Feng Guochang (1859-1919), the governor of Jiangsu, was a major figure within the Zhili Group of warlords. He suceeded Li Yuanhong as president in 1917.

10. The Guangxi warlord, Lu Rongting.

11. Marshal Cao Kun (1862-1938), a Zhili warlord, bribed members of the parliament to elect him as president of the Republic in 1923.

12. Soldiers of the Northern Army pose with their rifles.

13. Troops of General Wu Peifu, at Shan Hai Kuan at the eastern end of the Great Wall (1924).

14. The Manchurian warlord,
    Zhang Zuolin.

15. The Central warlord, Wu Peifu.

16. Feng Yuxiang, the 'Christian General', working on the construction of a dam in Shandong province (1932).

17. Feng Yuxiang (1882-1948) in dress uniform.

18. Zhang Zuolin in full military attire.

19. Feng Yuxiang with General Chiang Kaishek.

20. General Chiang Kaishek and Song Meiling (Madame Chiang Kaishek) in the garden of their country home in Guling (Lushan), Jiangxi province (before 1938).

21. The 'bandit' warlord, Zhang Zongchang, who ruled Shandong province between 1925 and 1928.

22. A Chinese armoured train with its Russian crew.

right wing at Rehe (Chengde). The Third Division held a line along the Tientsin–Pukou Railway, and this drew extra support from the various *dujuns* of central China, who had hitherto been sitting on the fence to see how General Wu would fare in an encounter with the re-armed and retrained Manchurians.

It seemed a fairly even match, but at least Wu was showing that Zhang Zuolin could be confined to Manchuria if only the Zhili forces had the resolve to do it. But on 23 October Feng Yuxiang betrayed Wu. Feng, who had been advancing north at a restrained pace to support Wu, suddenly turned round and returned to Peking in an amazing forced march, seizing control of communications and the police, and presenting Wu with a *fait accompli*. Feng imprisoned Cao Kun, who had bribed his way into the presidency the previous year. Wu Peifu's army, demoralized by this treachery, broke and ran, and Wu had to flee by ship with some of his crack units.

Wu Peifu could have foreseen such a move, because in 1923 Feng had already demonstrated the scope of his ambition as a kingmaker, if not a king, when he deposed President Li Yuanhong. But as has been noted already, Wu was weak in political guile and really only understood fighting and literature.

A new situation now prevailed, with China divided among the Kuomintang in the south, east China and the Yangtze basin under the warlord Sun Chuanfang, and Zhang Zuolin in control of Manchuria and the north-west and with a legitimate claim to a share of the government in Peking. Feng Yuxiang was roaming around as unpredictably as ever.

In November 1924, Wu returned to Luoyang via Zhengzhou. Despite his recent defeat, he was still a respected figure, and both Duan Qirui and Zhang Zuolin would have been glad to ally themselves with him to crush Feng Yuxiang. Instead, Wu spent much of 1925 trying to re-establish himself as leader of a coalition of central provinces — Henan, Hubei, and Hunan. He underrated the strength of the KMT forces in the south, and failed to see that he was simply setting himself up as the main warlord force to be defeated in the Southerners' drive on Peking.

The KMT's Northern Expedition got going in July 1926. Wu Peifu, whose forces had occupied part of northern Hunan, clashed with the KMT expeditionaries at two strategic bridges, but his troops broke and ran. Wu himself had to flee north and cross the Yangtze at Wuhan, the Southerners in hot pursuit. After unsuccessful assaults on the walls of Wuchang (one of the three cities making up Wuhan), the famous Communist general Ye Ting settled down to besiege the city, where the civilian population was soon starving and short of water. Wu and the rest of his army were pushed north out of Hubei and into Henan, while Wuchang surrendered after a six-week siege.

Chiang Kaishek's forces turned eastwards down the Yangtze to defeat the Nanking warlord Sun Chuanfang, and having chased him out of the city, rested there to take stock and plan the next moves. In the spring of 1927, friction between Chiang and the Communist and leftist commanders with their Russian advisers at Wuhan broke out in earnest, and Chiang ordered savage massacres of Communists in Shanghai and all over Southern China. However the military alliance of what were now two different command centres — Wuhan and Nanking — held. The Wuhan wing resumed its offensive up the Peking–Hankou Railway. Wu's subordinates were divided as to whether they should ally themselves with Zhang Zuolin or with Feng Yuxiang (who was coming out in favour of the Northern Expedition). In the paralysis of decision-making, Wu's force was overtaken by the Southerners and roundly defeated.

Wu and a few remnants of his once mighty army escaped westwards into Sichuan, where he was welcomed by Yang Sen and other local warlords. After enjoying their hospitality for five years, he went on to Gansu, in the north-west, where he became *honoris causa* commander of an independent army with a strong Muslim contingent which was still defying the authority of Chiang Kaishek. Assuming authori-ty over Shanxi province's Warlord Yan Xishan, Wu called for a combined attack on the province of Shaanxi and the rais-ing of his banner as commander-in-chief of a 'Chinese National Defence Army'. But their uprising was short-lived and Wu again had to flee. In 1939 there was talk of inviting him to accept a high position in the Japanese-backed puppet government in China, but he would probably have refused. Wu Peifu died in the same year.

Feng Yuxiang, the Christian General[8]

Feng Yuxiang was born in Zhili province (nowadays Hebei) in 1882. His parents were badly off and his father had joined the army to make ends meet. He enlisted the boy at the age of ten and father and son served together for several years until Yuxiang was accepted as a fully-fledged soldier. Impetuous and energetic, the young Feng foreswore early in life the habits of gambling and drinking alcohol, and took pleasure in the brisk monotony of military drill.

In 1902 he joined one of Yuan Shikai's guards units and rose steadily, attaining the rank of company commander within three years. Feng was transferred to the crack Third Division of Yuan Shikai's northern New Army and followed the colours to Manchuria. Suppression of bandit gangs and routine duties added to his experience, and he supplemented the meagre education of his boyhood with a private reading campaign including the Chinese classics and old chronicles of famous warriors and battles.

Under the influence of a brother officer, Feng became interested in the movement to overthrow the Manchus. He aligned himself with anti-Manchu elements among his acquaintances when the 1911 army mutiny at Wuchang in central China marked the beginning of the Revolution, and he narrowly escaped execution as a traitor.

When Yuan Shikai assumed the presidency of the Chinese Republic in 1912, Feng's military star rose once again and he was permitted to recruit a whole battalion. By 1913 he attained the rank of regimental commander. He won distinction in the campaign to hunt down the well-known bandit nicknamed the White Wolf, becoming commander of a mixed brigade in the process.

---

[8] The main source in English for the career of Feng Yuxiang is Professor James E. Sheridan's *Chinese Warlord: The Career of Feng Yu-hsiang*, Stanford: Stanford University Press, 1966.

Around this time Feng developed a curiosity about the doings of the Christian missionaries. Though Christianity had an obvious appeal to his puritanical nature, it may be that he also observed the advantages to be gained from being religiously linked to the ideological arm of the foreign powers, who were carving China up among themselves. Throughout his career Feng showed himself a strange mixture of idealist and cynic, ally and turncoat.

On 1 January 1916, Yuan Shikai had himself proclaimed emperor in Peking, whereupon the *dujun* of Yunnan province, General Cai E promptly declared independence and moved some of his troops into Sichuan to forestall military action against them from Peking. Feng Yuxiang was sent with one regiment of northern troops to Sichuan, but he dragged his feet and began negotiation with Cai E. Eventually he was forced to engage the Yunnanese in battle near Xuzhou, in southern Sichuan, but by private arrangement his troops and the Yunnanese just put up a show of firing at each other, though some casualties occurred on both sides.

After Yuan Shikai's death in June 1916, Feng was ordered by the new cabinet to station his men on the railway line between the capital and Tientsin. In the following year he refused to obey orders and lead his men to Gansu province, which had a problem of frontier defence. He was deprived by Peking of command of the Sixteenth Mixed Brigade, which he had come to regard almost as his personal property, but managed to stay in touch with its officers, who were loyal to him personally, in expectation that the command would revert to him at some stage.

He was right. In mid-1917, Zhang Xun attempted to restore the boy emperor Puyi to the throne. Feng and his men played an important role in suppressing the coup, and as a reward he was formally restored to his command.

Full-scale civil war was brewing up in central China. The warlord regime in Peking and other parts of north China was openly at odds with the Kuomintang led by Dr Sun Yatsen in the south. The North attacked Hunan province, the gateway to Guangdong, but the Hunanese proved tougher than expected, and even the Northerners' most capable commander, General Wu Peifu, was unable to occupy the province decisively. Wu soon tired of this irksome task and began requesting to be relieved, prior to peace talks.

If the Northern troops could not invade KMT-controlled Guangdong directly via Hunan, there was a possible invasion route through Fujian, the maritime province to the northeast of Guangdong. Premier Duan Qirui ordered Feng and his brigade to take that route. Feng, with astounding sangfroid, ignored the order and settled his troops at Pukou in Jiangsu province, the railhead just across the Yangtze from Nanking.

The Peking government again called on Feng — this time for another push against the Southern armies which were still holding onto most of Hunan province. Feng appeared to consent and shipped his brigade up the Yangtze as far as Jiujiang. Then his extraordinary insubordination took control again: he sent out an open telegram calling for peace and deploring the civil war. This mutinous behaviour nearly cost Feng his command, but he somehow bluffed it out and in April 1918 did lead his troops into Hunan and engage in fighing there. This brought him into the command sphere of Cao Kun, governor of Zhili and effectively commander-in-chief, as well as of Wu Peifu.

Feng was made defence commissioner of Changde — a town in Hunan which he had occupied in the course of his three months there. This gave him the opportunity to settle down for a while and test in practice the ideas of military and ethical training of troops which his mind had been working on for some time.

Feng's ideas were similar to those of a public-school headmaster of the time in England. He forbade his men to smoke tobacco or opium or drink alcohol, and made them study the Bible. But his ideas of military equipment were somewhat old-fashioned. James Sheridan writes:

One of Feng's units that attracted much attention in later years was the Ta-tao-tui [*dadaodui*: Big Sword Unit]. It was apparently established in 1917, though it may have been in existence earlier. It was initially called the Pistol Unit, and each man was outfitted with a rifle, a pistol and a large sword. The unit was manned by troops handpicked for their fighting ability, and in subsequent years their exploits, particularly with their flashing blades, made them respected and feared throughout China as the Big Sword Unit. They later accomplished heroic feats against the Japanese. As Feng's army came to include more than one brigade, each one apparently had its Big Sword Unit. The men of these units wore patches on their uniform that read: 'When we fight, we first use bullets; when the bullets are gone, we use bayonets; when the bayonets are dull, we use the rifle barrel; when this is broken, we use our fists; when our fists are broken, we bite.'[9]

Feng required his troops and officers to take part in sport, gymnastics, and gruelling route-marches. The illiterate were taught to read and write, and trained in trades so that they would not be destitute and turn to banditry when they left the army.

Feng's ethical training was mainly based on the elimination of bad personal habits and building of a patriotic morality similar to the Boy Scout movement in Britain. He looked on Christianity as a force for morale and discipline among his men, and told foreign missionaries: 'Remember that your chief work is not to try to convert the rank and file of my army, but to use your strength in trying to get all my officers filled with the Spirit of God, for as soon as that takes place, the lowest private in the army will feel the effects of it.'[10]

At this distance in time it is impossible to assess just how profound or sincere was the Christianity of Feng's men. Their virtues were extolled by a number of missionaries, but

[9] Sheridan, *Chinese Warlord*, p. 76.
[10] Jonathan and Rosaline Gosforth, *Miracle Lives of China*, Grand Rapids, 1933. Cited in Sheridan, *Chinese Warlord*, p. 83.

the missionaries' 'opiate' was optimism. As to opium itself, the US military intelligence attaché, Joseph B. Stilwell (later General Stilwell), observed that in Shaanxi province, of which Feng was made governor in 1920, coolies were still spending one-third of their daily income on the drug. He came to the conclusion that there would be 'a revolution' if Feng tried to ban the opium trade, which raised enough revenue for him to pay his men and even send some to Wu Peifu, who had no such ready source of funds.[11]

Whether out of religious belief or practical considerations of training and morale, Feng came closely in touch with his men, frequently stopping to chat with them about their living conditions and more general topics. He also reduced the incidence of beatings of men by their officers, and laid down rules which had to be complied with if a man were to receive corporal punishment: for instance, if he was a new recruit, or had just eaten, the officer should only use his own hands, not an instrument of punishment.

Feng encouraged the singing of 'improving' songs — much as the People's Liberation Army of today is taught to sing only 'healthy' songs about patriotism and love for the people. Mao Zedong, Feng, and the Shanxi warlord Yan Xishan all hit upon the startling discovery that common soldiers are human beings deserving of respect and more likely to give their best if well-treated. This was a somewhat shocking insight in a quasi-medieval country where soldiers were traditionally treated as cannon-fodder of no intrinsic worth, simply material to be pounded into shape, ripped to shreds, or thrown away when useless.

Even in the famous and popular chronicles of the deeds of great commanders, little is ever said in praise of the ordinary fighting man. No Chinese commander made it a routine practice to stroll among his men — 'a little touch of Harry in the night', as Shakespeare puts it in *Henry V. The Water*

[11] Barbara W. Tuchman, *Stilwell and the American Experience in China 1911–45*, New York: Macmillan, 1971, p. 78.

Margin, for that matter, which is supposed to represent the rejection of tyranny, invariably refers to the foot-soldiers in the outlaw band as *xiao lolo* — of which there is no real equivalent in English, but which can be roughly rendered as 'rabble'.

The other simple truth that Mao and Feng understood was that soldiers who respect the common people will enjoy their support or at least sympathy. Feng ordered all his men to settle up their debts with local tradesmen before breaking camp, just as Mao made sure his troops re-attached wooden doors on peasants' houses which they had borrowed to sleep on. The military value of such behaviour is of little account for a big army, which will be victorious or defeated on account of other factors than correct behaviour towards civilians. But there are always times when a little low-level intelligence can be gathered, short-cuts pointed out, and wounded stragglers taken care of until they can rejoin their units. An overall programme of self-improvement may give soldiers a sense of worth and self-esteem, which may improve their performance on the battlefield.

In 1920 the Anfu–Zhili War was fought, resulting in the defeat of the Anfu Group and its abandonment of Peking to Zhili forces led by Cao Kun and Wu Peifu. Feng joined the latter in fighting against the Anfu troops, and for this he received as a reward the military governorship of Henan province, his principal source of manpower recruitment and his home base if he could be said to have one at all. But he was frustrated by the lack of money and supplies, and on one occasion actually stopped a train bringing revenues to Peking and seized the money. In 1921 he was transferred with his mixed brigade to Shaanxi province. He became military governor there after assassinating one of his rivals for power at a dinner party, whilst another contender committed suicide. Feng's Christianity had taken on a distinctly Renaissance flavour.

After setting in train his usual social reforms in the province, which was plagued with poverty and banditry,

Feng came up against the problem of anti-foreign feeling, and it may have been his own professed Christianity that prevented attacks on missionaries in Shaanxi.

Feng's tenure in Shaanxi was brief. In 1922 he decided to participate in the first Zhili–Manchuria war, in which the Manchurian dictator Marshal Zhang Zuolin took on the Zhili forces headed by Cao Kun and Wu Peifu. Feng Yuxiang sent part of his troops — which had been redesignated the Eleventh Division — to help the Zhili Group, and Zhang was chased back beyond the Great Wall. Then Feng moved his men to the ancient Northern Song Dynasty capital of Kaifeng, in eastern Henan. Once again Feng started pushing his social medication, attacking vice, gambling, excessive taxation, bandits, footbinding, and bad roads.

Late in 1922, Feng was summoned by the Peking government to come to the capital and take on the duties of army investigation commissioner. His popularity in the country was immense, second only to Sun Yatsen's. However the move to Peking could mean a loss of real power, and the people of Henan were distressed by his early reassignment, since they could hardly expect any future *dujun* to treat them so well.

After the move to Peking, Feng had difficulty paying his army, which was mostly quartered outside the city at Nanyuan. Li Yuanhong, the man who had been forced to take the leadership of the 1911 Revolution in Wuchang, was reinstated as president. Feng supported a movement to oust him, and the President took refuge in the foreign concession at Tientsin. Law and order were breaking down in Peking, so Feng's army stepped in to restore calm. He partially solved his financial problems by gaining control of the salt octroi, a reliable source of revenue.

During the two years following his defeat at the hands of the Zhili leaders and Feng Yuxiang, Manchuria's overlord Zhang Zuolin had been working hard to upgrade and modernize his army, and by 1924 he felt ready to take on his Zhili enemies again. His plan soon became evident, and in

September 1924 Feng was ordered by Peking to take his army northwards to the Great Wall, while other Zhili troops would march on Shanhaiguan to prevent Zhang Zuolin from entering China proper.

When manoeuvres had been in train for about a month, Feng suddenly made an about-face and marched his troops back to Peking, capturing strategic points and seizing control over all communications, with the pre-arranged co-operation of the capital's garrison. He then broadcast an appeal for a peace conference, and the forces at his command were renamed *Guominjun* ('National People's Army').

Wu Peifu attempted a counter-attack on Peking, but was defeated and cut off from his main army at Shanhaiguan, and he and the remnants of his men fled down the coast by ship to the Yangtze basin to plan their comeback. Cao Kun blamed Wu for the fiasco; he himself was arrested and imprisoned in Peking by Feng.

After a peace conference in Tientsin, Duan Qirui was restored as premier and the Zhili–Manchuria war was officially ended. With characteristic unpredictability, Feng announced that he was going abroad, but for the meantime he set up headquarters at Kalgan (now Zhangjiakou), as he was entitled to do under his 1923 appointment as commander of defence of the north-west. By now both the KMT and their Soviet advisers looked on him as a promising ally, but physical contact with him was difficult.

Kalgan was certainly a good place for Feng to exercise his social and economic reforms. Once a thriving trading centre located between Inner and Outer Mongolia, the city had fallen into decline because of the unstable conditions in Mongolia and Central Asia, to say nothing of the ripples of the Bolshevik revolution in Russia. A European merchant described it thus:

> Kalgan lies three thousand feet above the sea and at the foot of the Mongolian plateau, two thousand feet higher up, and is reached by a steep pass from the West Gate, one of the few passes through the almost sheer escarp-

ment. It is surrounded by wild mountain scenery. There is a more or less straight main road leading to the North Gate where a dry river bed provides open-air storage for the traders' cargo, mostly wool, hides and skins. In this road shops are built on high embankments on both sides. Practically every other shop is a saddle shop, or displays riding gear and kit, riding whips and flywhisks, headstalls and the heavy iron stirrups of the border. Customers, mostly Mongols, in greasy plum-coloured or yellow robes, waddle painfully along, clearly out of their element, as they loath walking even a few yards, or doing anything that cannot be done in the saddle.[12]

Feng built new roads and planned to extend the Peking–Suiyuan Railway. He solicited loans from the Japanese, towards whom he was often friendly. But like every warlord he depended for his main revenues on the resources of the territory he ruled. He taxed grain, wool, cigarettes, and so on, monopolized all road transport in the north-west and opened a hotel and a bank. Feng attacked poverty and disease through social welfare programmes and free education. But all these reforms cost money, and well-intentioned as they doubtless were, they depressed the business climate. Feng had no scruple about using the north-west's opium as a source of revenue — indeed he ordered the planting of more of the profitable crop, according to one source.

Feng benefited by the poverty of the north-west in another way: he stepped up his recruitment programme until he had a force of some 100,000 men under his direct command. But most of the new recruits were Muslims, and would not submit to Christian baptism.

Feng had long shown a strong interest in the Russian revolution and Communism. He had little chance of contact with the Soviet advisers at Canton and Wuhan. But in 1924 Leo Karakhan, the first Soviet ambassador, set up his chancery in warlord-ruled Peking, not in revolutionary Canton — one of the first in a long series of Soviet blunders

[12] A.H. Rasmussen, *China Trader*, New York: Crowell, 1934, p. 195.

in treatment of China, which was continued by Stalin and Khrushchev and which their successors failed to repair to any great extent. In 1924 warlord troops stormed the Soviet embassy in Peking, arresting ensconced Chinese leftists, who were later executed by strangulation, and seizing secret documents including accounts of Feng's arms purchases from the Russians.

Feng had never given up the idea of visiting the Soviet Union, and the Russians were interested in wooing him as a potential ally. In the spring of 1925 they began transferring advisers to his army, but Feng strictly prevented them from engaging in political indoctrination of his men. None the less, the Russians began supplying him with significant quantities of modern small arms, and conventional military training by Soviet and other foreign instructors went ahead.

Receiving substantial aid from the Soviet Union as he was, Feng was again faced with the charge that he had been converted to Communism, a charge he vigorously denied, representing himself as first and foremost a Chinese patriot. And as though to emphasise his commitment to Christianity, in the face of both imperialism and Communism, he organized a corps of army chaplains to work among his men.

Inevitably, during Feng's Kalgan period, he was drawn into ever-increasing friction with his old enemy, Zhang Zuolin, the overlord of Manchuria, who considered Inner Mongolia and the rest of the north-west to be his territory by right. Indeed Zhang hated Feng so much that he even joined up with his other old enemy, Wu Peifu of the Zhili Group, to fight the Christian general. Feng, in view of the relative weakness of his army, avoided provoking Zhang or Wu and took up defensive positions in the north-west. But Wu attacked Henan with its pro-Feng army, and with the help of the local Red Spear peasant rebels threw out the pro-Feng *dujun*.[13] A cargo of Soviet arms for Feng on the ship *Oleg* was

[13] Societies such as the Red Spears were formed by peasants in areas troubled by armies and bandits to provide some self-protection. They were based in the folk religions and martial arts world from which the Boxers came.

captured by the Manchurian at Tientsin, and troops Feng had stationed there withdrew westwards. Meanwhile Feng courted popular support by expelling the boy emperor Puyi from the Forbidden City and inviting Dr Sun Yatsen to visit Peking.

In November 1925 Feng Yuxiang backed the dissident Manchurian general Guo Songling in his rebellion against Marshal Zhang Zuolin. Zhang put down the revolt with Japanese military assistance and had Guo and his wife summarily executed. This led to a direct conflict between Feng and the Manchurian army, with Wu Peifu moving up from the south to encircle the former. In addition, Feng's men were fired on by the Japanese when they started building fortifications at the old Dagu forts, demilitarized under the 1901 treaty which wound up the Boxer uprising. Japan presented an ultimatum, with the support of the Western powers excluding Germany. Feng's men were in danger of encirclement and in March 1926 they withdrew to Peking and garrisoned it.

Feng now took the decision to let the situation settle down on its own while he paid an extended visit to Outer Mongolia and the Soviet Union. In April 1926, Feng's forces near Peking took up strong defensive positions at the Nankou Pass, near the capital, and dug in for a long siege. It fell to Wu Peifu to attempt to dislodge this tenacious force, which detracted from his ability to prevent the KMT army from fighting its way northwards to Wuhan and beyond — for by July the Northern Expedition had begun in earnest.

Feng had announced his resignation from the post of north-west defence commissioner on New Year's Day, 1926. He travelled slowly to Urga, capital of the Soviet-dominated Mongolian Republic (now Ulan Bator). He was impressed by the progress he saw there, and with a strange logical flip, let himself be persuaded to join the KMT through a message to Canton. Feng was given a warm reception in Moscow, where he met many Bolshevik luminaries, including Leon Trotsky, and was subjected to an intense barrage of Soviet propagan-

da, which duly impressed him. He signed for large arms purchases and returned to China in August 1926, as his troops
were evacuating Nankou in the face of overwhelming force
on Wu Peifu's side.

After five months' respite with his men in the north-west,
Feng moved through Shaanxi province to invade his old base
province of Henan in order to join up with the Northern
Expedition, whose troops had seized Wuhan and Nanking
and were preparing to launch the second phase of their drive
on Peking. But severe political splits between Chiang Kaishek
in Nanking and the leftists and Communists in Wuhan held
up progress, until Chiang ordered his savage massacre of the
latter throughout Shanghai and other KMT-controlled parts
of southern China. Feng had problems of his own in the
north-west, which was coveted not only by Zhang Zuolin in
Manchuria, but now also by Yan Xishan, the reforming *dujun*
of Shanxi, who had a strong interest in Inner Mongolia and
Suiyuan. By the end of 1926, however, Feng had most of his
remaining forces in Shaanxi, where they were able to relieve
the city of Xian from a cruel and ruinous siege by an odd
combination of warlord troops and peasant rebels from
Henan.

While preparing for his invasion of central China to link
up with the Southerners' expeditionary force, Feng stepped
up the politicization of his troops, using both Soviet methods and his own tried and tested techniques. But he could
not fail to be aware of the KMT–Communist split on the
Yangtze, and he kept a measure of political independence
rather than becoming wholly identified with the Soviets.
Whereas his previous indoctrination of the troops stressed
morality and self-improvement, he now shifted the emphasis to the mutual support of his soldiers and the peasants —
an early version of what Mao and his followers practised in
the areas under their control in distant Jiangxi.

The KMT–Communist split in 1927 put Feng's political
convictions to the test. In June he met leaders of the leftist
Wuhan faction at Zhengzhou, capital of Henan, which his

men had recently captured. Feng was at that time in a position of military superiority over the other northern warlords except Zhang Zuolin, so it was easy for him to win consent to his occupation of Henan. He also acquired decisive political influence in Gansu and Shaanxi provinces, and could eye Shandong speculatively.

Next on the agenda was a meeting with Chiang Kaishek, between whom and Feng there was no love lost. However conferring in Xuzhou, a strategically located town in Jiangsu, they declared their hostility to the northern warlords and their loyalty to Dr Sun Yatsen's ideas. More important, they agreed that the Soviet adviser Borodin and his assistants should leave China, a move which poured cold water over Feng's alleged friendship with Moscow. Now moving visibly towards an anti-Moscow stance, Feng purged Communist agitators in areas under his control — mostly without bloodshed, by contrast with Chiang Kaishek's massacres of Communists in the south.

Feng's apostasy as a follower of Lenin did not seem to be rooted in any deep ideological change in his outlook, but rather in opportunistic considerations concerning the extent of his personal power. Perhaps at the last moment he foresaw what a danger it would put him and his armies in if he became formally labelled a Communist: this would have been an invitation to the Western powers and Japan to give aid to anyone who happened to be fighting or challenging him. The sympathy Feng commanded among foreigners on account of his Christian faith was helpful to him, and despite the Soviet arms supplies he could not afford to be written off now as a Bolshevik. It should also have been evident to him that the Wuhan regime was a lame horse to back, the likely victors of the civil war being Chiang Kaishek and — Feng had grounds to hope — himself.

If Feng had initially been carried away by the Soviet Union, the Russian advisers at Canton were equally enamoured of him through the reports they received from

Moscow and from northwest China. This could only alienate Chiang Kaishek, who was touchy and jealous of his leadership position in the revolutionary movement. The Communist general Zhang Guotao noted:

> In February, 1926, when Feng was fighting against Chang Tso-lin [Zhang Zuolin] and Wu P'ei-fu [Wu Peifu], Kisanko (the chief Soviet adviser in Canton) and his colleagues had blatantly recommended to Chiang [Kaishek] that he send his troops by sea to Tientsin to give Feng Yu-hsiang [Feng Yuxiang] support. They even wanted Chiang to go north to undertake the training of cadres for Feng Yu-hsiang. Such proposals clearly betrayed an ignorance of the concepts of a Chinese military leader. Chiang wanted to create a world by himself; how could he be expected to play second fiddle to Feng? One can readily understand how he would nurture the feeling that the Soviet Union was not attaching importance to the National Revolutionary Army [that is, the KMT forces] in Kwangtung [Guangdong], and was intentionally snubbing him personally.
>
> It was, however, a doubtful point whether the Soviet Union really wanted to suppress Chiang. ... The responsible comrades of the CCP Kwangtung District Committee informed me that Borodin and the Soviet military advisers held Chiang in higher respect than Wang and that surely they could not have any intention of suppressing Chiang. But the Soviet people had attached too much importance to Feng Yu-hsiang's 'coup in the capital' in 1924. They were anxious to change the status quo of the Peking government so that the Chinese revolution could achieve a phenomenal development that would benefit the foreign relations situation of the Soviet Union. And so they naively requested Chiang Kai-shek to send his armed forces to the North to make some spectacular accomplishment. After the departure of Borodin these 'village bumpkin' type Soviet militarists had had to undertake

the duties of diplomacy, and their political methods
were apparently so crude that they aroused Chiang's
reaction.[14]

In mid-1927, Feng's troops were drawn into the complex
stalemate in which the Northern Expedition had become
trapped. Feng clashed with warlord armies contending for
possession of Xuzhou, in Jiangsu. With his help the
Southerners' expeditionary army was able to consolidate its
positions along the Yangtze, and they received a further fil-
lip in 1928 when Yan Xishan, the Shanxi warlord, joined the
expedition (his men were actually the first to enter Peking).

In the spring of 1928 Feng's men — including tough, fast
cavalry recruited in the north-west — clashed with Manchurian units which had reached the northern borders of
Henan, and penetrated Shandong. The war was now a free-
for-all, with regiments and army corps fighting hundreds of
miles away from their home provinces. The net closed quickly around Peking, and Marshal Zhang Zuolin, who had been
heading an administration there since 1926, left for
Manchuria by rail. Japanese agents blew up his train and
killed him as he neared Mukden.

One of the main tasks facing the victorious Nationalists in
1929 was the disbanding of the regional warlord armies.
Feng Yuxiang ostensibly agreed to go along with this, but
like the others he merely took cosmetic measures and kept
the real strength of his army intact in Henan. None the less,
he accepted a position as chairman of a committee for military disbandment.

In his latest base of Kaifeng, Feng once more set about
implementing his reform policies, including — with a particularly modern twist — censorship of erotic or over-violent
films. He also tried to attract members of the Red Spears peasant rebel bands, who had so fiercely besieged Xian three
years previously. Campaigns to abolish foot-binding were

---

[14] Chang Kuo-t'ao (Zhang Guotao), *The Rise of the Chinese Communist
Party*, Part I, Lawrence: The University of Kansas Press, 1971, pp. 496–7.

carried out in areas under his control, especially in Shaanxi, 'where officials were particularly diligent and advertised their success by hanging discarded foot-binding cloths before the government buildings, where they made a gay sight'.[15]

A White Russian officer, Colonel Anatol M. Kotenev, has left this portrait of Feng at the height of his power:

> Marshal [Feng Yu-hsiang] sincerely believed in the righteousness of his course of action in exposing the vice of his contemporaries, and, no less sincerely, he desired to keep his army intact: the only true National Army capable, in his opinion, of leading China along the path of moral and material regeneration ...
>
> Of huge stature, robust and a little clumsy in his soldiers' grey cotton uniform and worn-out shoes, and without any sign of his high rank, he presented a unique figure among the military and civil officials of modern China. Plain and outspoken, sometimes even violent in his language, he was the only one of the military leaders who lived as a common soldier and underwent all the toils and hardships of a soldier's life. One could see him riding a bicycle followed by his orderlies; wheeling a barrow of earth, with a member of his staff pulling it long with a rope in front — for all the world like a couple of coolies. His regular meal as well as that of his officers and men consisted mostly of steamed bread and cooked unpolished rice ...
>
> In 1923 Feng Yu-hsiang, as a member of the Ashbury Methodist Church in Peking, was elected as the Chinese Delegate to the General Conference of the Methodist–Episcopal Church, which was held the following year in Springfield, Massachusetts. However, some unforeseen political development prevented him from attending.

Feng's recruits received obligatory baptism, but he laughingly denied rumours that he performed it with a fire hose to speed the process. Kotenev recalls:

[15] Sheridan, *Chinese Warlord*, p. 245.

Bible study was a part of the daily programme. Morning and night the tunes of hymns were wafted on the air over the encampments. Every conceivable spot on the walls on which characters were likely to attract the eye was utilized for the painting of mottoes and Bible texts urging the soldiers to Repent and enter the Kingdom of Heaven, to love their country, father and mother, wife and children, etc. A 'Christian Council', consisting of chaplains, directed and supervised the work of evangelization. It was planned to have a chaplain for every 1,000 men, Marshal Feng Yu-hsiang playing the leading role as preacher and Minister. He never missed a chance to address his men and to rouse their religious and patriotic enthusiasms.

Another of Feng's ways of educating his men was to keep them busy at all times.

There were all kinds of workshops where they were taught useful trades, weaving, carpentry, and so on, so that, when discharged, they could support themselves. There was also a thorough education course and all were expected to learn to read. Education was not only compulsory for the soldiers but also for the wives and families of Officers who resided in garrison quarters. If the latter refused to enter upon a course of instruction they were packed off and sent to their homes without ceremony. Facilities were also provided so that Officers and men could save money. A military bank was established for this purpose. Every soldier had an account, and he was expected to deposit his monthly pay retaining only one silver dollar for personal expenses. This bank undertook to remit money to home addresses in all the northern and north-western provinces, and the regular arrival of such proofs of filial piety and consideration for the old folks evoked grateful astonishment in the villages.[16]

However, more serious problems such as famine, banditry, and excessive taxes were undermining Feng's authority in

[16] Anatol M. Kotenev, *The Chinese Soldier*, Shanghai: Kelly & Walsh, 1937, p. 114.

Shaanxi, Gansu, and Henan, the provinces he controlled. In addition, a Muslim revolt broke out in Gansu, with horrible massacres of civilians, and the inevitable processions of destitute and dying refugees.

Feng's alliance with Nanking did not last. In the late 1920s relations between Feng and Chiang Kaishek deteriorated. Feng blamed Chiang for not allocating sufficient funds to his army, and Chiang accused Feng of damaging national unity. Feng and his most loyal subordinates declared war on Nanking; the KMT government promptly 'dismissed' him from his posts and put out a warrant for his arrest.

On the other hand, Feng had been cultivating better relations with Yan Xishan, the *dujun* of Shanxi, and they even talked aloud about going abroad together. But they found potential allies against Chiang Kaishek among the KMT leftists who had survived the purge of 1927 and who were openly trying to unseat him again. Fearing opposition on too many fronts, Chiang attacked Feng's army round Luoyang, in Henan. Yan Xishan uncharacteristically committed himself to the fight, his troops penetrating as far as Shandong to distract Chiang, whose headquarters were still in Nanking. In July 1929, the various forces opposing Chiang conferred in Peking and elected Yan and Feng and the leftist Wang Jingwei as leaders of the rebel faction. In an unexpected twist, Marshal Zhang Xueliang of Manchuria — son of the assassinated Zhang Zuolin — expelled Yan's Shanxi troops from Peking and allied himself with Chiang Kaishek. Feng, unable to cook up any new coalition to challenge the KMT leadership, abandoned control of his army and went into seclusion.

Feng devoted himself to a programme of reading and self-improvement, but burst into public life again in 1933 when the Japanese invaded Manchuria in strength. He raised an army of several thousand men and called it the People's Anti-Japanese Allied Army, with the avowed aim of attacking the invaders when Chiang Kaishek would not. Taking Chahar as his base, Feng attempted to form an effective modern army, but the patriotic organizations which offered support were mostly too lacking in military training to be of much use. They did, however, score some initial victories by attacks on the Japanese rear, although Feng did not succeed in setting up a unified command, and when the Japanese turned round to face the scratch force, it melted away, and Feng returned to his place of retirement at Mount Tai, in Shandong, a centre of Daoism.

Over the next three years he often sallied forth with speeches calling for the Chinese people to unite against the Japanese. Chiang Kaishek, however, was still obsessed by his desire to wipe out the Chinese Communists, who in 1935 arrived in the north-western province of Shaanxi at the end of the Long March from Jiangxi.

Full-scale war with Japan broke out in 1937, and Feng lent his political weight to Chiang Kaishek and the national cause, following the KMT leadership to Chongqing in Sichuan province and remaining there until the defeat of Japan in the Pacific War.

In 1946 Feng went on a prolonged visit to the United States, during which his public pronouncements became increasingly hostile to Chiang Kaishek, and he announced his intention of setting up a rival party on the grounds that Chiang had betrayed the principles of Sun Yatsen. He set sail for home on a Soviet ship. On 5 September 1948, the Soviet authorities announced that he had been killed in a shipboard fire — arousing suspicion but affording no proof that he had been assassinated. His widow went on to serve in high positions in health and child welfare work for the new Communist government in China, which gave Feng ritual honours and put his ashes to rest at his beloved Mount Tai.

3   The Western Warlords

Li Zongren and the Flying Army[1]

THE PROVINCE OF Guangxi has a special mystique in the Chinese consciousness. The tall, steep-sided mountains of Chinese brush-painting — which to many foreigners seem to be mere products of the imagination — are there found in real life. Their rocky flanks clad with scrubby trees, bushes, and creepers, they soar out of the rice-paddies like so many indistinctly-carved chessmen, stretching to the horizon in all directions.

These mountains, composed of limestone karst, set limits on Guangxi's suitability as a place for human habitation. They are, for one thing, quite useless, unless some of the vegetation at their feet be cut for firewood. They govern the twists and curves of the few roads. Their monotony, however inspiring to the artist, bestows a feeling of oppression, helplessness even. They seem to belong to an alien planet of some distant solar system, not to the earth as we know it. If man seems dwarfed in the karst landscape, his activity is also curtailed by the appalling, humid heat of the southern climate hanging over the entire province for six months of the year. In winter, by contrast, it is chilly, sometimes wet, and misty near the coast of the South China Sea. In the west, Guangxi borders on Vietnam; to the east is the rich and populous province of Guangdong. To the north and west are the mountainous, barely accessible provinces of Yunnan and Guizhou.

[1] The main text on Li Zongren in English is Diana Lary, *Region and Nation: The Kwangsi Clique in Chinese Politics 1925–1937*, Cambridge: Cambridge University Press, 1974.

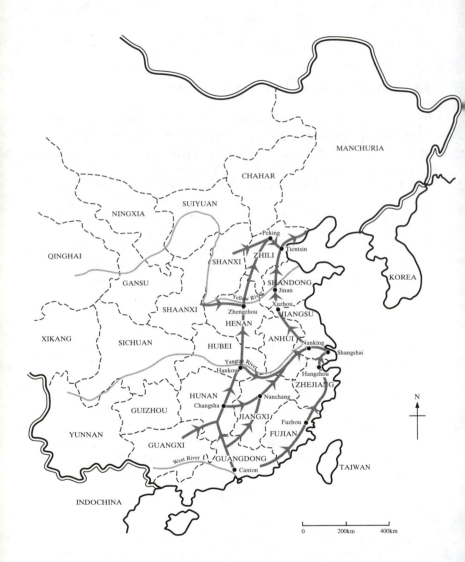

Main lines of the Northern Expedition, 1926–7.

The people are of mixed origins, some speaking a form of northern Mandarin, some Cantonese — the language of Guangdong — some the Hakka dialect, others again talking the obscure languages of ethnic minorities: Miao, Yao, Zhuang, and others. The Zhuang — a people loosely related to the Thais — are the most numerous, estimated at some eight million in the early 1980s, but largely assimilated into the ethnic Chinese who populate most of the province. The people of Guangxi are notorious for their fractiousness and hostility to strangers.

In 1916, Guangxi's governor, a former bandit called Lu Rongting, attempted to expand his territory by invading the neighbouring province of Guangdong. For the next few years, Guangxi was involved in sporadic wars with Guangdong and mutual occupation of each other's territory. Lu was ostensibly loyal to the revolutionary leader Sun Yatsen, who visited the province twice, but he had actually no idea of the KMT's wider aims of reform and national reunification. After Lu's second defeat in 1921, much of his army dissolved into roving bands, closely linked to banditry. The bandit problem in Guangxi was particularly severe. A French missionary, the Reverend Joseph Cuenot, wrote that when bandits were in the offing, Chinese officials brought their wives and valuables to Christian missions for protection.

> Whenever there was a branch of the Red Cross, they gave a substantial donation which, they felt, permitted them to affix the Red Cross emblem on the door of their homes, and thus claim the protection of the civil authorities. It would be a simple matter to name villages where there was not to be found a water buffalo, pig, chicken, dog or cat after the departure of the robbers. Everything had been eaten. At times men even feared that their own bodies might enter the stomachs of the bandits. All know the Chinese custom of eating the heart and liver of those who have been shot or executed. A former bandit, living near the Catholic mission in

> Kweilin [Guilin], related that in 1923, near the district
> of Sau Yau, the bandits killed their captives because the
> ransom was not forthcoming, and that the bodies, cut
> and salted, were exposed to the sun for some time. After
> this treatment the meat was ready for broiling, and was
> then put on the menu.[2]

In 1924 Lu was finally overthrown and the provincial capital of Nanning occupied by the forces of a young officer, Li Zongren, and his colleagues. Li, the man who was to restore order in Guangxi and become the province's most famous son, was born near the beauty spot of Guilin in 1891, the son of a village schoolmaster. After a patchy education, he enrolled at the provincial military school. Following service in a crack fighting unit known as the Model Battalion, Li became an independent commander of an area of seven counties on the Guangdong border, where he was eventually joined by a friend from officer training school, Huang Shaoxiong. As the rest of the province descended into petty warring among local commanders, Li and Huang ran a tight ship in their area. In 1924 they peacefully occupied Nanning while the provincial overlord was besieged by rebels at Guilin. The latter's troops fled to French-ruled Tonkin (Vietnam) and a few months later Sun Yatsen, at his Kuomintang headquarters in Canton, recognized Li, Huang, and their ally Bai Zhongxi, as the rulers of Guangxi — henceforth known as 'the Kwangsi [Guangxi] Group'.

In 1926 Li and his colleagues agreed to enrol their armies as Kuomintang troops, though they themselves kept control of their men in Guangxi. A wave of nationalistic, anti-foreign fever was sweeping China at the time. Foreigners' property was destroyed. A Soviet adviser was sent to Guangxi, and Li's forces were renamed the Seventh Army Corps, and joined the KMT's Northern Expedition.

---

[2] Joseph Cuenot, *Au Pays des Pavillons Noirs*, Hong Kong: Imprimerie de Nazareth, 1925, pp. 52–3.

The Guangxi troops' first major clash with the Northerners was in Hunan province, where the local warlord had been defeated by the invading forces of Wu Peifu from the north. Hunan was too close for comfort to the KMT headquarters, then still located in Canton. Wu was driven back, and Hunan's troops were enrolled in the KMT's National Expeditionary Army. Li and the troop under his command marched on the big Yangtze city of Wuhan, and in August 1926 roundly defeated Wu Peifu again, taking the city.

The Soviet advisers Borodin and Blyukher (alias Galen) installed themselves in Wuhan together with Communist elements of the National Expeditionary Army, who were ostensibly collaborating with and under the orders of the KMT. Wang Jingwei, the leftist revolutionary who later became a Japanese puppet, was also in Wuhan. Borodin attempted to persuade Li Zongren to come over to the Communist faction. He was by now a famous and popular general and the Seventh Army Corps — variously nicknamed the Flying Army and the Army of Steel — was of great importance to the future of the Northern Expedition. But Li stood firmly on the side of Chiang Kaishek, who had launched an offensive eastwards into Jiangxi province with the aim of capturing Nanchang, Nanking, and Shanghai.

Over the protests of the Russians, Li decided to march down the left (northern) bank of the Yangtze in support of Chiang to deal with the Nanking warlord Sun Chuanfang, leader of the League of Five Provinces in eastern China. (The five were Zhejiang, Fujian, Jiangsu, Anhui and Jiangxi.) Though Chiang Kaishek suffered a bad check at Nanchang, capital of Jiangxi province, Li pushed on, defeating Sun Chuanfang in three successive battles.

When the Northern Expedition took Nanking, its soldiers killed several foreigners, and others barely escaped with their lives. Chiang Kaishek, Li Zongren, and other KMT leaders could sense the danger of the foreign powers intervening militarily if there were further such incidents and if the

Communists based at Wuhan continued stirring up trouble in the big cities — especially foreign-dominated Shanghai. Historian F. F. Liu writes: 'Li's army was the only outfit not seriously infected by the Communist influence. He and his [Guangxi] associate, Pai Chung-hsi [Bai Zhongxi], shared a soldier's suspicion of the motives of the Communist International in China. Having been assured of their support, Chiang had Li's [Seventh] Corps redeployed in the Nanking area, and, in a master stroke, purged the Communists from the First Divisions of his own army *à la pointe des canons* of the Kwangsites [Guangxi troops].'[3]

Bai was himself an outstanding commander, and a significant measure of Li Zongren's success is to be laid at his door. A graduate of the Baoding Military Academy, he was a member and staunch supporter of the Kuomintang. He played an important role in the bloody suppression of Communists in Shanghai in 1927, and was among the first commanders to enter Peking victoriously in the following year.

On 12 April the KMT began to purge all Communists from its ranks, beginning in Shanghai, where execution details with huge broad-swords roamed the streets, killing any worker or student who looked as if he might be a Communist. Chiang then ordered the Wuhan faction to get rid of the Soviet advisers and expel the Communists from the faction there.

In August 1927, Li and other commanders beat off a strong Northern attack on Nanking, and from then on their effective power in the Northern Expedition was consolidated. Gloom descended over Wuhan and its Soviet advisers. Mrs Borodin had been detained when Shandong troops searched a Soviet liner which put in at Pukou, near Nanking. The Soviet Embassy in Peking was broken into and searched on the orders of the Manchurian warlord Zhang Zuolin, who was temporarily in control of the capital. Twenty revolu-

---

[3] F.F. Liu, *A Military History of Modern China*, Princeton: Princeton University Press, 1956, p. 47.

tionaries, including Li Dazhao, one of the founders of the Chinese Communist Party, were strangled in Peking. The Soviet advisers left Wuhan despondently for home.

The Wuhan faction had seen Chiang's action against the Communists as having been taken in response to pressure from, or even in collusion with, the imperialist powers. Zhang Guotao, the pro-Communist general who was in Wuhan at the time, writes in his memoirs:

> Certain important personages of Wuhan held that Chiang Kai-shek, Chang Tso-lin [Zhang Zuolin] and even the diplomatic corps in Peking were coordinating their efforts for unanimous action. That it had been possible for the men with real power, such as Chiang Kai-shek and Li Chi-shen [Li Qishen, a Guangxi general] and Li Tsung-jen [Li Zongren] to join forces against the Communists was not only due to the efforts of the imperialists behind the scene to bring them together, but also was only possible with their actual support. Such things as the shaky position within the ranks of Wuhan and its economic difficulties were also the result of manipulations by the imperialists.[4]

As the Northern Expedition proceeded, Li Zongren remained in the rear to take over the administration of Wuhan through one of five branch political councils set up by the KMT to control China's five main cities. But in January 1929, he sacked Nanking's appointee to the Hunan provincial commitee, which was under the general command of Wuhan. Fearing retribution, Li uncharacteristically fled to Shanghai. The KMT government dismissed him and two of his closest Guangxi associates from all their positions and expelled them from the party for life. Such was Li's reward for his previous aid to Chiang Kaishek.

Back home in Guangxi, Li again became embroiled in quarrels with the province's eastern neighbour, Guangdong.

---

[4] Chang Kuo-t'ao (Zhang Guotao), *The Rise of the Communist Party, Part I*, Lawrence: The University of Kansas Press, 1971, p. 593.

His aircraft dropped some bombs on Canton, the provincial capital. Hunan province got in on the act by invading northern Guangxi. It was a typical warlords' mess. Li later said in a speech:

> We are still sunk in the chaos of warlordism. The nation's peril increases daily, and society becomes increasingly disturbed. What is the reason for this? It is entirely due to the lack of psychological reconstruction, to the pervasiveness of self-seeking. ... When they [the senior officers] started out, though they wanted to work for the nation, they found themselves in a corrupt environment, surrounded by an atmosphere of self-seeking, tainted and misled. They could not resist it.[5]

During the 1930s, Li and his colleagues increasingly turned their attention to the internal administration of Guangxi, and in the opinion of some authorities made an outstanding success of it. Though militaristic and anti-intellectual (he even disliked music), there was a rough integrity in Li. Like many of the warlords, he and his colleagues admired early European Fascism as the answer for a once-proud nation humbled by internal dissension and external weakness. But his overall attitude was of a Confucian stripe, and his frustrated patriotism showed, perhaps, in his admiration of Edward Gibbon (1737–94) and his monumental historical work, *Decline and Fall of the Roman Empire*.

Li maintained good relations with Guangdong after the 1929 fighting, and often visited Canton. He was also to be seen in British-ruled Hong Kong. As a result of Chiang Kaishek's refusal to devote all his resources to the encroaching Japanese in the early 1930s, instead of attempting to liquidate the Communist stronghold in Jiangxi, the commanders in Guangxi and Guangdong became increasingly hostile to Chiang's policies and whipped up a fever of anti-Japanese feeling in their provinces. They were regarded as model patriots by many people in other parts of China indignant at the

---

[5] Lary, *Region and Nation*, p. 157.

Japanese inroads. The crowning achievement of Li's military career was his victory over Japanese forces at Taierzhuang, in Shandong province, in 1937, after full-scale war between the two countries broke out. Chiang, realizing for once the desirability of making use of Li's military experience instead of quarreling with him, appointed him director of the KMT Fifth War Zone.

Under Li's overall command, a Chinese army attacked a division led by General Isogai Rensuke, despite the Japanese preponderance in armour and vehicles. Li pursued encirclement tactics and pinned the Japanese down at Taierzhuang, a small town on the south bank of the Grand Canal. Japanese tanks reached the walls and a rain of shells poured into the town where the Chinese made their stand. Chinese soldiers took the tanks on with grenades and anti-tank guns, but still the Japanese advanced. A massive artillery duel ensued and the Chinese brought their planes up to bomb the Japanese lines. A Japanese reporter said fighting the Chinese was 'like chasing flies'. The Chinese commanders on the spot appealed to Li's headquarters in Xuzhou for permission to withdraw, but Li refused on pain of court martial. Cooks and porters were ordered to join in the fighting. The Japanese were reduced to using tear-gas to defend themselves, and several hundred who had barricaded themselves into one corner of the town were smoked out or killed in a single action. The Chinese pressed the attack with hand-grenades and swords. Japanese casualties in the entire battle were put at 20,000 (other reports say 30,000). The Chinese success was attributed to close-in fighting at night, which the Japanese were not used to. Some reports ascribed the victory partially to the German adviser von Falkenhausen, who followed the battle from Nanking. Japan lost two of its best divisions and suffered an important moral blow.[6]

The victory at Taierzhuang enabled the KMT government to consolidate its position around Hankou, following the

[6] Dick Wilson, *When Tigers Fight: The Story of the Sino-Japanese War 1937–1945*, London: Penguin, 1983, pp. 94–110.

evacuation of Nanking before the advancing Japanese. But Chiang Kaishek, with characteristic ineptitude, virtually retired Li after this brilliant success, and the old soldier spent the rest of the war grumbling at his enforced inactivity.

Li made a brief comeback in 1948, when he was elected vice-president in opposition to Sun Fo, son of Sun Yatsen. But he was unable to exercise much influence on Chiang Kaishek, who was rapidly losing ground to the Communists, and as the latter approached Peking, Li left for the United States. In 1965 Li caused a sensation by returning to Communist-ruled China and was enthusiastically welcomed by the Party and government, who used him to encourage other former KMT notables to rally to the national cause regardless of their politics. He died in 1969, in the middle of Mao Zedong's Cultural Revolution.

Yan Xishan in Shanxi[7]

The most truly modern figure among all the warlords, Yan Xishan showed the influences of European fascism and Russian Bolshevism, Japanese militarism, Confucianism and Christianity, and the Boy Scout movement. Some of his attempted reforms were reminiscent of the methods later put into effect by Mao Zedong.

Yan's social experiments in the northern, land-locked province of Shanxi were wide-ranging and are known in considerable detail through the descriptions of visitors, but most especially through the lectures he gave and through his own writings. The available material has been admirably assembled and collated by the American scholar Donald G. Gillan. Gillan was also able to interview Yan in person during his twilight years in Taiwan.

The character of Shanxi is defined by its geographical orientation towards the grasslands of Mongolia and Ningxia, with their semi-nomadic herdsmen living off the produce of their dairy animals (including mares as well as yaks, goats, and sheep). No longer a military menace in themselves, the Mongols and ethnic Chinese Muslims (Hui) live mainly off mutton and dairy products, millet, and wheat imported from China proper. Their products are mostly sheepskins, leatherware, and rugs, as one can still witness today on the streets of Shanxi's most famous city, Datong. Here there are magnificent giant rock-carvings of Bodhisattvas left behind by the Toba Wei, a central-Asian race who ruled parts of China in the period towards the end of the fourth and the beginning of the fifth centuries AD. Shanxi is also an important centre for Tibetan-style Buddhism, though there are relatively few Tibetans in the province and the big monasteries mainly attracted Mongol and Chinese monks.

---

[7] The major study of Yan Xishan in English is Donald G. Gillan, *Warlord: Yen Hsi-shan in Shansi 1911–1949*, Princeton: Princeton University Press, 1967.

As has been noted, Shanxi is a major coal-producing area, and this is both a strength and a weakness for anyone who rules it. Coal was essential to China's modern industrial development from the late nineteenth century onwards, and the province's rich resources made it a tempting prize for the Peking and Nanking governments of the 1920s, and later the Japanese who annexed Manchuria in the 1930s. (The American tycoon Armand Hammer co-operated with the Chinese government in the mid-1980s to open the biggest joint venture the country had ever known — an open-face coal-mining facility at Pingshuo, near Taiyuan.)[8]

Shanxi is mainly surrounded by mountains to the east, south, and west, and there are only a very few passes though which an effective invasion can be launched, unless it be by the northern grasslands which were called Suiyuan during the warlord period. Yan Xishan put the province's natural defences to good use and rarely took his armies campaigning in other parts of the country, something which undoubtedly helps to account for his long tenure as governor.

Shanxi was famous for its bankers and merchants, and it was into a family of the latter than Yan Xishan was born in 1883, not far from Taiyuan. When he was an adolescent he was enrolled in military college, then sent for two years to Japan — the favoured course of training for a soldier's career in early twentieth century China. As a brigade commander in the Chinese imperial army, he defected to join the revolution in 1911 and soon became established as governor of Shanxi, receiving his marshal's baton from Sun Yatsen himself. In the deadly minuet of the warlords, Yan favoured the Manchurians, War Minister Duan Qirui, and Wu Peifu's Zhili Group to resist — or sometimes co-operate with — the Christian General, Feng Yuxiang.

Yan proceeded to create a provincial army with officers trained either at Baoding or at the provincial academy. His troops were of a relatively high standard: they were mostly

---

[8] This co-operation came to an end after the death of Hammer in 1992.

local men, something which always raised the morale of warlord armies, who hated fighting far from their home province. They had a reputation as good shots, for alone among the warlords Yan insisted they be trained with live ammunition. In addition, they were subjected to a large variety of morale-building and self-strengthening programmes devised by Yan. His military reputation was high enough for the Communists to agree to let their most experienced commander, Zhu De, serve if only nominally as his second-in-command for a while in 1940, during the Anti-Japanese War which was supposed to be a period of Communist–KMT collaboration. On the other hand, the Communists were able to induce five of Yan's crack 'dare to die' regiments to defect to their side, so socially motivated had they become.

Shifting alliances were characteristic of Yan's tactics, even more so than was normal among the warlords. He was sometimes allied with, sometimes waging war with, Feng Yuxiang, the Communists, and the KMT forces. From early in his career he had enjoyed considerable popularity in China as a whole. An English-language magazine polled its readers as to whom they considered to be the greatest living Chinese. Yan came ninth; the first three names were Sun Yatsen, Feng Yuxiang, and Wellington Koo (the sometime foreign minister).

Yan's most constant preoccupation was to keep Shanxi free of any armies but his own. Geography came to his aid in this, but the area he fully controlled was whittled down over the years until towards the end, his writ ran in only about one-eighth of the province's area.

In the 1920s, Shanxi attracted a good deal of attention for Yan's socialistic policies, and he was widely referred to as 'the model governor'. However, he depended on excessive taxation for his schemes and by the 1930s he had run Shanxi, once a stable and prosperous province, into financial ruin, with the accompanying evil of famine. The fact that he was alternately trying to stave off occupation of Shanxi by the Kuomintang government in Nanking, by the Communist armies from the south, and by the Japanese through Inner Mongolia did nothing to stabilize his situation.

One perspicacious observer of conditions in Shanxi was Harry A. Franck, an intrepid American globe-trotter who visited the province in 1923. He also interviewed Yan Xishan at this relatively early stage of the latter's programme of reforms.

After a nightmarishly uncomfortable train journey from Peking, Franck alighted in Taiyuan, the capital of Shanxi. Along the way he had witnessed the booming coal industry in action — Shanxi being one of China's biggest coal-mining areas — mostly from open-cast pits. The use of coal in pre-modern China was fairly restricted because of traditional beliefs. Franck writes:

> Some of the old superstitions that made delving in the earth so unpopular still prevail. Evil spirits guarding these hidden treasures will wreak vengeance on the men who dare to disturb them — and, what is worse, on the whole community. Dragons are still known to spit death-dealing vengeance on those who dig too deeply for coal; in other words, there have been cases of fire-damp explosions ... and many of the miners themselves still think that coal will grow again in an empty shaft within thirty years, and iron and gold in longer periods.[9]

Franck found Taiyuan a somewhat lackadaisical place, with the slowest rickshaw-pullers in China. 'Taiyuan labors under the handicap of three kinds of time, "railway," "gun", and "university" time. The last is considerably slower than either the station clock or the governor's noon-gun, and rumour has it that it gradually became so because the curriculum included a number of eight-o'clock classes which certain of the most influential faculty members could never

    [9] Harry A. Franck, *Wandering in China*, London: Fisher and Unwin, 1924, pp. 259–61.

quite reach.' Yan Xishan also resented the slow speed of life in the city, and formed an Early Rising Society to make the people livelier.

The American traveller noted with approval that roads had been built to speed the province's development, although 'it is true that these roads are largely due to American famine relief under missionary management, and that the principal highway runs about two hundred li [60–70 miles] northward exactly to the governor's native village.' He also commented on the school-building programme, the removal of beggars from the streets, the campaign against opium, and the relatively hygienic aspect of the city brothel, with its 500 prostitutes.

Accompanied by a British-trained interpreter, the globetrotter paid his respects to the 'model governor' — a 'solid-looking man, with a somewhat genial face sunburned with evidence of his personal attention to his outdoor activities.' He gave an impression of practicality and personal lack of ostentation. But he was known to be stymied in many of his reforms by corrupt or idle officials, for instance in his campaign to eliminate the practice of foot binding.

On the streets Franck reported seeing public buses, and trucks running mainly on steam, for coal was much cheaper than petrol. The old city wall had been neglected, and was turning into a ruin, because from a military point of view it was useless to fend off bandit attacks. Since the soldiers and police actually received their wages regularly, they were relatively effective in suppressing bandits, whereas in most provinces the soldiers' wages were often unforthcoming, which drove regular soldiers into banditry.

Yan was working on the creation of a village militia made up of local people only. He showed a strong sense of localism, for instance in his refusal to commission any officers who were not natives of Shanxi. Franck learned that Yan was personally very rich, despite his modest dress, but none the less was popular with the people after twelve years of his rule: 'There are still such adversities as famine in Shanxi Province, and numbers of its men emigrate northward to Mongolia and Manchuria in search of the livelihood their ancestral homes deny them. But even a civil and military governor combined cannot make rain fall.'[10] The excitement-loving American's chief complaint about Taiyuan was that it was boring!

In 1924 Yan assisted in the defeat of Wu Peifu, who was at war with Feng Yuxiang and the Manchurian forces of Zhang Zuolin. His denial of supplies to Wu came at a crucial moment, and it would have been logical for him thereafter to join the pro-Manchurian alliance of northern and eastern warlords, but he preferred to stay at home in Shanxi. The year 1926 found him fighting his erstwhile ally, Feng Yuxiang, for control of northern Shanxi. This was after Feng had tried to lure Yan into an alliance, hoping thus to tip the balance of power in north China in his own favour. Yan had evidently seen through Feng's plan to occupy the area of Datong, an important rail junction. Feng and Yan eventually settled their differences when Yan agreed to let Feng's troops along the Peking–Suiyuan Railway.

In 1926, impatient with Yan's fence-sitting in the face of the advancing Northern Expedition led by Chiang Kaishek, with his mainly south Chinese troops, Manchuria's overlord Zhang Zuolin declared war on the Shanxi leader; relatively little fighting ensued, however, and Yan remained in control of most of his province. In the following year, Yan accepted the title of commander of the Third Army Group of the KMT forces, and played a role in the massed advance on Peking by occupying Shijiazhuang, an important city in Zhili province (now the capital of Hebei).

New Year's Day (Western style) of 1929 saw Yan participating in the work of the newly set-up Military Disbandment Committee. Chiang Kaishek had decided that with the occupation of Peking and the rout of the Northern

---

[10] Franck, *Wandering in China*, p. 264.

warlords in 1928, it was time to consolidate his power by whittling down the strength of the various regional armies which had assisted, with differing degrees of enthusiasm, in the success of the Northern Expedition. Though the committee decided in little more than three weeks to divide China up into four 'disbandment areas' — one of which was Shanxi — none of the warlords took these proposals seriously. Yan, with some 200,000 men under his command, had no strong motive to disperse them, whatever Peking (now renamed Beiping or 'Northern Peace') said.

Throughout 1929, Chiang's authority was increasingly challenged by Feng Yuxiang and his 'Christians', and while Yan did not concur immediately in a proposal to join an assault on the new KMT capital of Nanking, he remained aloof from the fighting between Feng and Chiang Kaishek in late 1929 and early 1930.

Suddenly, in February 1930, Yan dispatched several telegrams to Chiang Kaishek, calling for his resignation, suppressed KMT government institutions in Shanxi, and had his men seize the Tientsin customs office. He was recognized as the leader of the anti-Chiang Kaishek movement, with Feng Yuxiang as his deputy. The pair set up an anti-Nanking government at Beiping (Peking) in the summer, and the enraged Southerners, seeing the fruits of the Northern Expedition about to be enjoyed by others, hit back in strength through central China. Zhang Xueliang, son of the assassinated Manchurian leader Zhang Zuolin, denounced Feng, used his own troops to occupy Beiping and other important places in north China, and turned them over to the KMT.

Despite his part in the mutiny against the KMT government at Nanking, Yan restored his rule in Shanxi in 1931. For the next decade and more, his main military preoccupation was with the Japanese, though he also fought their common enemy, the Communists' Red Army, and sometimes clashed with KMT forces. His central aim was to keep such 'foreigners' out of Shanxi.

Originally the Japanese threat to Shanxi was of an economic nature. Mass-produced Japanese goods outsold their Chinese competitors with their more primitive manufacturing facilities. The traditional Shanxi bankers were driven out of business because they failed to move with the times and adopt modern methods of money-management. Japanese moves to bring Manchuria and what is now Inner Mongolia under their suzerainty presented a constant threat to Shanxi's northern borders, which were hard to defend. And in a modernized version of China's old opium problem, the Japanese were illicitly shipping large quantities of morphine and heroin into the country, which may have contributed slightly to a decline in national morale.

The near-total opportunism of Yan's political and military tactics can be seen in the shifting relations he maintained with other power centres. When the Japanese left his territory alone, he maintained good relations with them. When the Communists were near at hand, he collaborated with them — though in the 1920s he had sent some of his own troops to help the KMT encircle the Jiangxi Soviet areas.

Years later, Yan collaborated with the Communists, actually taking nominal command of the famous Eighth Route Army, with the Communist hero Zhu De as his second-in-command (but this was thought to be merely a courtesy extended to Yan as a symbol of collaboration of Chinese forces against Japan). The force under Yan's command attacked the Japanese at Taiyuan in 1938. Only two years earlier, Yan had had to call on Nanking for aid against a Communist force led by the legendary Peng Dehuai, which was campaigning in southern Shanxi. But with the breakdown of Communist–KMT collaboration at the end of the Second World War, Yan allied himself with Chiang Kaishek and fiercely attacked the Communists, using captured Japanese troops.

Shanxi's main natural resource is coal, but Yan never managed to provide sufficient reliable transport for it to be shipped to other provinces. Despite Yan's attempts to establish self-sufficiency in heavy industry, consumer goods, and so on, silver flowed out of the province to purchase goods not in local supply. The currency declined, and Shanxi became a food-deficit area.

The main fault in Yan's economic experiments was that he carried nothing through to a conclusion. Like Mr. Toad in *The Wind in the Willows*, he was carried away with some bright idea while the last one was left to crumble from neglect. And like every warlord, his solution to economic problems was taxation ever more and more taxation. He taxed weddings and funerals, wealth and profits, land, cigarettes, and liquor (perhaps because of his opposition to smoking and drinking).

By the 1930s unemployment was rife in Shanxi, but Yan, inspired by the experience of the Soviet Union, continued with poorly prepared schemes to introduce a form of socialism. He strengthened the police force, invented slogans to replace old good-luck sayings, and tinkered with the idea of the abolition of currency and payment in 'product certificates'. And like the leaders of modern Russia, but unlike those of modern China, he wanted to increase, not control the growth of population.

The 600-mile long railway Yan built to link northern and southern Shanxi certainly improved matters, though its skimpy construction and narrow guage limited its usefulness. The motor roads were so badly built that they quickly fell into disrepair and were not systematically worked over. And he never succeeded in quelling the landlords who squeezed the peasantry to their last drop of sweat.

The relative ineffectiveness of Yan's reforms was emphasized by the relative success of those carried out by the Communists in neighbouring Shaanxi province, to the south, and in parts of Shanxi which they occupied from time to time. Within a year after 1937 the Communists and their sympathizers acquired control of most of the territory left unoccupied by the Japanese.

The vacillating and opportunistic stance adopted by Yan during his extraordinarily long domination of Shanxi is exemplified by his shifting relations with the Feng Yuxiang. The two warlords kept a sort of mutual balance in north China, but they also fought each other on several occasions, maintaining none the less a degree of mutual respect. Yan at one stage offered to go on a world tour with Feng, if it would help to settle some political problems in China. The combination of these two was a source of irritation to Chiang Kaishek, and when the German military adviser General Georg Wetzel arrived in 1930, he identified the Feng–Yan relationship as needing to be neutralized by military means. Chiang, absorbed in the attempt to encircle the Jiangxi Soviet areas, paid no attention to Wetzel's advice.[11]

Chiang Kaishek, as has been amply demonstrated elsewhere, was so obsessed with the need to put down his former partners, the Communists, that he underrated the importance of Japanese inroads into Chinese territory and the chronic instability caused by the marching of warlord armies back and forth across the land and the leeching of the country's resources by their enemies.

Yan accepted high-sounding titles from the KMT government at Nanking, and made a show of loyalty to Chiang Kaishek, but actually he ignored most of Nanking's instructions and directives. He usually tried to avoid large pitched battles, but in 1937 he fought alongside KMT troops and Communists to defend the provincial capital Taiyuan, inflicting heavier casualties on the Japanese than they had suffered anywhere in China so far. But with his territory reduced to a part of southwest Shanxi, Yan later collaborated with the Japanese to keep up pressure on the Communists entering Shanxi from the adjacent province of Shaanxi, where they had their Yan'an base.

American journalist Harrison Forman described Yan's role in the Anti-Japanese War as follows:

> The Japanese seemed not to press Yen [Yan] too hard, and there was more than a suspicion that they regarded

[11] Jerry Seps, 'General Georg Wetzel', in Bernd Martin ed., *Die deutsche Beraterschaft in China, 1927–1938*, Dusseldorf: Droste, 1976, p. 113.

> Yen as a possible successor to the Generalissimo should
> Chiang Kai-shek be defeated. ... He was thought of not
> necessarily as a puppet but rather as a compromise
> between the extreme of treason at Nanking (the pro-
> Japanese puppet government headed by the former
> KMT leftist, Wang Jingwei), and national resistance at
> Chungking [Changqing, in Sichuan province, seat of
> Chiang Kaishek's wartime government].[12]

After the defeat of Japan in the Pacific War, Yan continued
his private war against the Communists, using captured
Japanese soldiers under General Imamura Hosaku. The end
was inevitable, even though Yan tried to bluff it out. As
Donald Gillan described it:

> About this time there appeared in the American maga-
> zine *Life* a photograph of Yen [Yan] seated at his desk
> contemplating a pile of capsules filled with cyanide,
> which he swore that he and his followers would swallow
> before they surrendered Taiyuan to the Communists.
> The Communists charged that as part of an earlier cam-
> paign to impress Americans and persons in other parts
> of China, Yen invited a group of foreign and Chinese
> newsmen to visit besieged Taiyuan and induced them to
> lavish praise on his regime by giving them precious gifts
> and setting them up in a brothel at the expense of the
> provincial government.[13]

Shanxi fell to the Communists in April 1949. Yan had
already fled to Nanking in March — predictably taking the
province's gold reserves in his plane. Chiang Kaishek gave
him high government posts, but he was powerless to end
Chiang's feuding with President Li Zongren, who had retired
in a huff to his home province of Guangxi in south-west
China.

Yan followed the KMT leadership to Taiwan, where he
lived a life of semi-seclusion. He wrote several books, one of

[12] Harrison Forman, *Report from Red China*, New York: Henry Holt, 1945,
p. 31.
[13] Gillan, *Warlord*, p. 287.

which, with unconscious irony, was entitled *How to Impede War and Establish the Foundation of the World Unit* — this from a man who spent most of his life fighting or preparing to fight with his neighbours and others, and stubbornly defending his own province as though the rest of China was of little account.

Nevertheless, there is no question of the sincerity of Yan's attempts to modernize Shanxi, one of the more backward of China's provinces. He stood for things which nowadays are taken for granted but in the China of his day were highly controversial: abolition of foot binding, peasant militias, work for women outside the home, universal primary education. His interference in the lives of his subjects went so far as exhorting men to copulate more often with their wives, in order to put whores out of business. He inveighed constantly against smoking, drinking, opium, gambling, and the work-shy. Despite these modern ideas, his rule was strict and he was no sentimentalist when it came to executing anyone he considered to be an anti-social element. Like many men who wield great power, he was paranoically afraid of assassination, and he amassed a great fortune. At the same time, he despised corrupt officials and magistrates and tried to curb their excesses of squeeze and graft. He kept in touch with ordinary people's problems, especially early in his career.

Without committing himself to any particular religious belief, he was tolerant towards Christianity and Confucianism, but hostile to Buddhism. He stood for education of the masses, and proclaimed that 'the three great duties of the people are to serve in the army, to pay taxes, and to receive an education.' In some ways he resembled the dictatorial first emperor of China, Qin Shihuangdi, with his emphasis on standardization of weights and measures, compulsory military service, physical training, and a strong campaign of indoctrination centred on a process called 'heart-washing', which was something less than brainwashing, but something more than the Boy Scout's Oath.

Of all the major warlords — with the possible exception of

Liu Xiang in Sichuan — Yan was the most committed to his province and to the welfare of its people. But he was a dilettante in the art of government and instead of helping them he bankrupted them. Interestingly enough, Shanxi in the 1960s became the site of one of Mao Zedong's most utopian experiments — the 'model brigade' of Dazhai, which was supposed to be the model for the rest of China's peasants to emulate. Bitter toil and egalitarian incomes were the ideal. After Mao's death the experiment was scrapped and most of China's peasants reverted to private farming. Only there were no landlords any more.

Free-for-All in Sichuan

The provinces of Sichuan, Guizhou, and Yunnan make up a single geographical entity in west and south-west China. Sichuan is ringed with mountains and almost its only practical means of communication with other parts of China used to be the overland routes to Yunnan and Guizhou and the swift and dangerous Yangtze River, along which its trade with the rich down-river provinces of east China was, and to a great extent still is, conducted. Inside its mountain walls, Sichuan is one of the richest and most beautiful of China's provinces, with abundant resources of rice and bamboo, tea, silk, and many other products. In past ages it was dubbed the 'Heavenly Kingdom' and was, indeed, ruled as a single kingdom at various periods of dynastic decline in the Chinese empire. The people are considered shrewd and clannish.

Neighbouring Guizhou and Yunnan are both mountainous provinces inhabited by a score of ethnic minorities besides the Han Chinese. The geographical origins of the Miao, Yi, Naxi, and Buyi may be obscure, but in general it is accepted that in prehistoric times they were forced out of south China by the Han encroaching and settling from the north, and had to retreat into the mountains to escape persecution or genocide.

The history of the region is marked by rebellions and massacres, and because of Yunnan's proximity to Vietnam and Burma, it has always been subject to foreign influences — most recently those of the French, who in the nineteenth century had hopes of extending their rule over Indochina to Yunnan. The French priests and bishops were diligent throughout the whole of south-west China, converting people to Catholicism.

Yunnan can claim credit for being the first province to rebel against the rule of Yuan Shikai, when the former president of the Chinese Republic tried to have himself enthroned as emperor in 1915–16. The military governor of Yunnan, Cai E, who had imbibed some modern ideas, declared his province independent. To consolidate his position, Cai invaded Sichuan, the shortest route to the central China plain. After bitter fighting, the local warlords decided that Yuan's career had come to an end, and they declared Sichuan independent. The Yunnanese forces, however, were in no hurry to evacuate the opulent province, and even when they eventually withdrew from Chengdu considerable numbers remained in the hills and made forays from time to time.

A British consul-general, Meyrick (later Sir Meyrick) Hewlett, had recently been assigned to Chengdu, which as most travellers agreed was at that time (as capital of Sichuan) one of the most spectacular cities in China. Thanks to his memoirs there survives a lively account of the war among the troops of Sichuan, Yunnan, and Guizhou. Officers from Yunnan and Guizhou were doing what they could to establish some sort of civil order in Chengdu, the local warlords concentrating mainly on an attempt to exterminate each other. Into this situation stepped Hewlett, a man of enterprise and courage with no small opinion of himself.

Foreign consuls in those days were incredibly powerful in China. They communicated on terms of equality and even intimacy with warlords and officials. They mediated between provincial factions, tipped the balance here and there with promises of support, made protests and representations when their country's interests were at stake or their nationals were considered to be at risk, and if necessary whistled up gunboats to settle things in the simplest manner. Many of them were fluent in Mandarin and local dialects. Her Britannic Majesty's Chinese Consular Service was a career posting with its own language course. Some of these men, understandably, became pompous and arrogant; others acquired a deep knowledge of China and the Chinese language, and a lasting affection for her people.

Having previously served in Peking (and survived the siege of the Legation Quarter there in 1900), Hewlett had worked in Yichang, Changsha, Shanghai, and Hankou before being posted to Chengdu. Before leaving for Sichuan, he briefly met Cai E, the Yunnan commander who had been the first to mutiny against Yuan Shikai. Cai, who was terminally ill with cancer of the throat, was on his way to Japan to seek treatment.

The Englishman's description of Chengdu is worth recalling. 'No wheeled vehicles were allowed into the city,' he writes.

> The mode of conveyance was by sedan-chair, and the chair coolies of Szechwan [Sichuan] were famous. The main streets of the city were stone-paved, wide and flanked by shops on either side completely open to the road. All the shops displayed their shop-signs on large boards of scarlet or black with gold Chinese characters on them, the effect in the main streets was of passing through a long arcade of Oriental beauty. This effect was heightened in summer when the streets were sheltered by straw mats on huge erections of bamboo poles to protect them from the sun. Unpaved side streets ran in parallels connecting the main streets, and in these most of the residences of the wealthy residents of Ch'eng-tu [Chengdu] were located. Silk was in profusion, Szechwan silk being deservedly famous. There were streets with shops selling nothing but furs, brass shops, copper shops, medicine shops with rare native medicines of every sort, curio shops, jade, amber, silversmiths, priceless embroideries — a paradise for the lover of beautiful things.[14]

Chengdu was divided into three parts: the Chinese city, the Manchu city, and the imperial city. The city wall was about eight miles in circumference and an average of thirty-five feet in height. Its lines, according to legend, had been marked out by a water-turtle in ancient times. The Manchu city housed the Imperial Bannermen (soldiers). The imperial city was built inside the Chinese city, and was pretty and

---

[14] Sir Meyrick Hewlett, *Forty Years in China*, London: Macmillan, 1943, p. 89.

tranquil, filled with flowers and trees. Chengdu was often called the Hibiscus City.

This picture of beauty and harmony was rudely shattered shortly after Hewlett's arrival in 1916. Sichuan was at that time ruled by the governor of Yunnan, and the new consul-general learned of the severe friction between the people of the two provinces — the problem being, in the Briton's words, 'Szechwanese conceit and Yunnanese arrogance.' On top of that Sichuan was rich in resources, whilst Yunnan was poor (and to a large extent depended on the export of opium to other parts of China for its revenues).

At first the local Sichuan warlords had welcomed the Yunnanese and sided with them in declaring independence from Peking. But the overbearing manner of the Yunnanese troops had soured the feelings of the Sichuanese, and matters were complicated by the fact that Guizhou province had also sent troops to Sichuan.

Guizhou, despite resources of timber and minerals, is grindingly poor and historically has served as a place of refuge for the defeated in civil wars. Its military and civil governors were at that time in Sichuan, seeking an alliance of the three provinces to resist suppression by Peking's armies, and doubling as Sichuan officials.

On 18 April 1916, latent tensions between the Sichuanese and Yunnanese resulted in the stopping of an ammunition train, and fighting broke out. 'Many brutalities were perpetrated', writes Hewlett,

> ...and none who were there will ever forget the massacre on the East Wall where Yunnanese seized civilians and the police at the East Gate, whom they had disarmed, pressed down their heads into the embrasures of the city wall, then one stab on the back of the neck, and dead or dying, the victim was tossed over the wall — for days the marks of blood on each embrasure told its tale.[15]

[15] Hewlett, *Forty Years in China*, p. 94.

The Sichuan troops were led by an able young general, Liu Cunhou. The streets were heavily barricaded, but Hewlett clambered over the piled-up furniture to visit the Sichuanese commander-in-chief and the civil governor, Dai Kan, a Guizhou man. A ceasefire was agreed on, but it did not stick and there was furious firing all round which lasted until the next day. The Guizhou troops succeeded in separating the Sichuanese and Yunnanese, and the ceasefire went into effect. For his pains the British consul received a commemorative silk banner; one of his achievements had been to persuade the Sichuan chief-of-staff that there could be a ceasefire, if the position of two Chinese characters on a map could be changed to save the face of the Sichuan men. Less than a week later, the Yunnan troops left Chengdu, but the Guizhou peacekeepers remained. Dai Kan stayed on as military governor, but three months later the Sichuanese attacked his men and he committed suicide.

Hewlett later described a terrible fight which took place in September 1920 in the open country around Chengdu. A mere 4,000 Yunnanese troops attacked 16,000 Sichuanese. Driven back to the foothills, 700 of them stripped to the waist, or altogether, and charged the Sichuanese with knives and revolvers. The latter panicked and fled. Hewlett recalled:

> About ten of these heroes, for heroes indeed they were, were captured, naked as they were, kept in the streets on show in cold drenching rain before being murdered. Two were killed and cut up in the streets and I saw the hearts and livers hanging in a cook-shop. Two others were wrapped in wadding and burnt alive in the public park before a huge crowd of men, women, and children. Two others were taken to a temple; their shoulders were slit and candles put in. They were forced to kneel at the altar when the candles were lit, and on the flame reaching the bare skin, were hacked to pieces. I called on the Commandant of the City Guard and pleaded for the other prisoners who were incessantly being tortured, making holes in shoulders, back and even head and

inserting candles being common. I told him I considered the men were heroes, and deserved care; they were
under orders, and it was the men who sent them to fight
who deserved punishment. He merely laughed and said:
'Very well, Kuan San [Hewlett's Chinese name], we all
know your love of humanity and I will give orders there
are to be no more tortures.'[16]

Sichuan's relative isolation from the rest of China turned
the province's political movements inwards rather than out-
wards during the warlord period. Garrisoned by troops sup-
posedly loyal to Peking, but periodically invaded by Yunnan
and Guizhou, it knew little peace. It has been estimated that
between 1911 and the Second World War some four hundred
wars, big and small, were fought in Sichuan. None the less
the province succeeded in maintaining a considerable degree
of internal autonomy, if not unity.

For most of the warlord period the province was split into
half-a-dozen districts under military rule. Of these, the
Chongqing district under General Liu Xiang was the most
powerful because it dominated the commerce of the upper
Yangtze, maintaining extensive trading links not only with
other parts of Sichuan and Hubei, but also on the lower
stretches of the river with the teeming delta region and the
port of Shanghai. By the early 1930s, Sichuan was ruled by
Liu Xiang in the east; by Liu Cunhou in the north-east,
adjoining Shaanxi; by Tian Songyao in the north, adjoining
Gansu; by Deng Xihou in the north-west, adjoining Qinghai,
and by Liu Wenhui in the south-west, adjoining Xikang and
Yunnan. In a small central enclave, Yang Sen was enclosed
by the territory of Tian and the two Lius.

There had been considerable disorder in Sichuan following
the death of Yuan Shikai. The province had previously
declared independence, but centralized rule was lacking. The
Sichuan-born district governors fought each other more
often than they fought outside forces, and rarely crossed the

---

[16] Hewlett, *Forty Years in China*, p. 126.

border into other provinces. The common people held them in disdain or in fear, and nicknamed them with such sobriquets as Rotten Melon and Crystal Monkey.

Liu Xiang was born in 1889, into a family of modest means which secured enough basic education for him to enter a military school, where his academic performance was among the worst. Later in life many people who encountered him, including foreigners, commented on the seeming mediocrity of his mind and imagination. The fact remains that as a warlord ruling an important part of a large province for two decades, his record at the end was not to be despised.

Liu, like others of his classmates at military school, rose quickly through the command chain of the provincial army (later armies) in the sporadic warfare of the decade following Yuan's death. By 1926 he had established a relatively strong army based in Chongqing, and his chief preoccupation from then until his death was to hang on to it, and on to the power it bestowed.

The standard of troops in Sichuan in the 1920s was below that of many other warlords' men. The American writer Graham Peck described them thus:

> They swarmed along the road and through the adjoining country without any sort of order. Some wore uniform coats or hats, but the remainder of their costumes were dictated by individual tastes and means. All were armed with the traditional umbrellas and carried as well numerous washbowls, teakettles, flashlights, towels, uncooked vegetables, and extra sandals — these were slung over their shoulders or tied to their coats with twine. Many who had guns swung their smaller effects in cloths tied to the gun barrels in Dick Whittington style. Those who could afford to rode in sedan chairs or rickshaws, and those who had pets — dogs, birds, monkeys — carried them or led them on a string.[17]

[17] Graham Peck, *Through China's Wall*, Boston: Houghton Mifflin, 1941, pp. 170–1.

The armies were financed to a large extent by taxes levied on grain, salt, and opium, as well as other products of everyday use, and special levies. Chongqing's position on the Yangtze made it possible for Liu Xiang to tax goods travelling both up and down river. Military officers themselves went into business. Liu himself was not regarded as enriching himself through his high position, surprising though it may seem, and he enforced strict military discipline in most matters while turning a blind eye to the rackets run by his subordinates. His regular troops were unable to cope with the banditry that was found throughout the rural areas, and the local militia units sometimes exacted as much from the peasants as the bandits did. The disruption of the economy through civil war drove more and more ordinary workers into banditry. None the less, Sichuan was accounted less afflicted by banditry than many other provinces. The active programme of urban construction and road-building pursued under Liu Xiang provided jobs even when the harvests failed.

Yang Sen was the most flamboyant of the Sichuan warlords. Nicknamed 'Rat Face' because of his small mouth, he had decided to clean up Chengdu, the former provincial capital which was the main city of his rather small territorial holding. Without a by-your-leave or an apology to the residents, he dispatched axe-welding workers to chop down every building felt to be encroaching on what should be the street, as he planned to permit motor-cars to enter Chengdu. Owners and beggars competed with each other to seize the debris. Yang had the streets paved with flagstones so that rickshaws — almost unknown till then in western China — could circulate freely. (One of the common forms of passenger transport in Sichuan was a modified wheelbarrow, pushed by a coolie, in which people travelled quite long distances if they could not afford a litter or a mount.)

Chengdu had one amenity which every warlord wanted: an arsenal (built with funds originally earmarked for a mint). Our old friend One-Armed Sutton (see Chapter 2) had helped set it up before he was employed by Marshal Zhang Zuolin in Manchuria. (Sutton fled Sichuan after shooting dead a local commander who tried to assassinate him.)

Crime was so rife, according to the American traveller Harry Franck, that officials grimly joked about the possibility of innocent people suffering summary punishment by beheading: 'We can't make a mistake nowadays, for everybody steals.' Soldiers deserted frequently, and Franck saw two unfortunates who had been foolish enough to ask to leave the service. They were lying on the street recovering from the injuries inflicted on them with bamboo canes, the commonest disciplinary measure in China.

> Their thighs, from the waist to below the knees, were like raw beef-steak, swollen to more than twice the natural size, the blood-red skin seeming ready to burst with the pressure from within. ... I saw them there two days later, still lying on their dirty mats, curs now and then sneaking up to sniff at them. They would get well in time, no doubt, unless filth complications set in.[18]

Other unfortunates were the Manchu Bannermen who used to garrison the city, but who were disbanded after the 1911 Revolution. As former soldiers, they had no craft or trade with which to earn a living. Some had been killed or committed suicide. Others had taken to begging, as none of them were over-fond of work. The Peking government was supposed to pay them a stipend, but even in the capital the payments were hopelessly in arrears, and many of the Manchus went to paupers' graves.

Chengdu was an opulent and luxury-loving city despite the poverty of many of its citizens. But Sichuan as a whole was in a state of decline. For a province so rich in peacetime, the economic depression induced by civil war was a pitiful sight. The warlords taxed famine-stricken peasants sometimes years in advance. The civil government was weak and

---

[18] Harry A. Franck, *Roving Through Southern China*, New York, The Century Co., 1925, p. 552.

unstable. There were no railways, and the wages of coolies as a transport force were seven times the estimated cost of shipping by rail if a railway existed. (The first was built in 1928.) There was no motorable road between Chengdu and Chongqing, a distance of some 400 km. Commerce was conducted along the Yangtze and its tributaries.

Most of the warlords lived in ostentation and luxury. One had eight wives or concubines, all trained in tennis, so that there was always one ready to play with him when he felt like a game in his glassed-in court. An air of comic opera hung over many of their doings. Peck reported: 'General Liu [Xiang] was a typical old-style warlord; though he was progressive enough to like ice-cream and drive a Packard, he nevertheless relied in all decisions on the advice of a soothsayer known as Fairy Liu [a better translation would be 'Liu the Immortal'], who read the future in the entrails of animals.'

When the Northern Expedition led by Chiang Kaishek against the warlords got into its stride in 1926, the Sichuan leaders including Liu Xiang decided to throw in their lot with the Southerners. From Peking they had experienced only interference and invasion, and they were no friends of the east China warlords, especially Sun Chuanfang, who presided over an economic system partly devoted to soaking up the riches of Sichuan through the riverine route down the Yangtze to Shanghai. In the event, however, Sichuan troops made little contribution to the Northern Expedition's success — their main assistance having been to abstain from war against the expeditionary army. Liu Xiang's positive attitude towards the KMT surprised even the followers of Chiang Kaishek, who had previously considered him just another ruthless warlord. Actually the pragmatic Liu had probably sized up the situation and decided he had more to lose by resisting Chiang's armies than by welcoming their successes. For one thing he needed to be on the right side of whoever occupied Wuhan in order that riverine trade should not be disrupted. And Chiang could not force him to commit his troops to the field in central China, however many compliments they paid each other.

After the success of the Northern Expedition in 1928, the KMT government issued a grandiose proclamation about the integration of Sichuan into the Republic and reforms to be carried out there. Liu and the other Sichuan warlords simply ignored this, and no coercive organ of the Nanking government, nor any KMT soldier, was allowed into the province. The grand currents of national politics which swept around the main cities of China's anti-foreign demonstrations and the organization of militant trade unions and student movements were less felt in Sichuan, though certainly they made their appearance. Liu Xiang, after initial wavering, came down on the side of Chiang Kaishek and wiped out all Communist Party activity in the Chongqing district.

But this did not mean that Liu was submitting totally to the KMT: he merely kept their representatives in Sichuan down to a small number and restricted their activities. He and the other provincial commanders utterly ignored Chiang Kaishek's call for a reduction of troop strengths all over the country once the Nanking government had been set up. Nor did it increase the KMT's hold over Liu Xiang that Chiang bestowed high-sounding posts on him; he had most of the power he needed already.

In the 1930s, Sichuan had a serious problem of Communist military activity to handle. The Red generals Xu Xiangqian and Zhang Guotao had established a soviet or Communist enclave in northern Sichuan in late 1932, having withdrawn from their previous position in central China. This force was militarily significant, estimated at between 60,000 and 100,000 men. Its suppression could not be left to local commanders and militias. The Communists had begun their usual programme of indoctrination of the peasantry, land reform, easing of tax burdens, and adult education. Disunity and fighting among the Sichuan warlords gave them respite from attack, and within a year they had established a considerable territory under Communist rule and captured arms and ammunition in large quantities from

Sichuanese units. This served to unify the various district commanders to attempt to organize an effective strike force to be used against the Communists. But they failed to press any attack home, though they did reoccupy some of the territory the Communists had seized.

Meanwhile Liu had fallen under the influence of the necromancer Liu the Immortal, who gave the troops rousing pep-talks but was unable to bring victory in battle with his spells. The people of Sichuan were intensely superstitious, and those in the new Soviet area thought the Red leaders were reincarnations of famous rebels, or wielded mysterious powers. They were also very ignorant of conditions in other parts of China, regarding their home province virtually as an independent kingdom. Words like 'Communist Party' were taken to be powerful incantations.

The fighting in the area had ruined the economy of the northern Sichuan soviet, and famine was waiting in the wings. The warlord troops had soaked grain stores with paraffin (kerosene) to make the grain unusable, and there was an acute shortage of salt. Most of the troops' rifles were primitive and easily damaged, and there were not enough for even half the men. Clearly it was going to be no easy job to hold on to the soviet. The Communist commanders were in touch with Mao's headquarters in Jiangxi by radio, but probably fear of intercepts made communications guarded and difficult to interpret.

In November 1934, after the Japanese seizure of Manchuria, Liu left Sichuan for the first time in his life to discuss the crisis with Chiang Kaishek in Nanking. Typically, Chiang was more interested in suppressing the Communists in Sichuan than in resisting the Japanese. In return for aid and supplies, Liu had to accept the strengthening of the Nanking government's organs and authority in Sichuan. With Mao Zedong's forces approaching south-western Sichuan on their celebrated Long March to north-west China from the Soviet areas in the mountains of Jiangxi, and Xu Xiangqian and Zhang Guotao ensconced until early 1935 in their soviet in northern Sichuan, it was certainly arguable that the Communists posed a greater security problem for Sichuan than did the Japanese.

The Communists on the Long March may not have been planning to settle permanently in Sichuan, but they were there in sufficient strength for Liu Xiang and the other provincial warlords to feel obliged to let Chiang Kaishek send 20,000 KMT troops into the province and set up a new provincial government at Chongqing in 1935. As the military leader of the Chongqing district, Liu retained his positions and his army, whilst the other five district commanders had to surrender theirs to the national command. But whereas Liu was strengthened militarily by these moves, his powers as a civilian administrator were soon undermined by KMT officials sent in or appointed by Nanking. Sweeping financial reforms were introduced on a province-wide basis, and Liu Xiang was able to take a percentage of the new revenues for himself. The KMT seem to have tolerated this in the interests of avoiding conflict with him. Chiang Kaishek visited the province in March 1935, and was well received by the local people. Sichuan's old isolation was being broken down.

Liu Xiang and Chiang Kaishek could hardly rule Sichuan jointly for ever. Tax burdens became heavier, corvée labour was imposed. Military expenditure rose. The bandit problem became worse. KMT agents spread pro-Chiang propaganda among the peasants and soldiers. Drought, floods, and famine descended on the common people. Speculation and graft added to the burden of suffering. Relief funds sent by Nanking were diverted. None the less Liu Xiang continued to put on a show of support for Chiang Kaishek.

Mao's army, following a crucial conference among the leaders at Tsunyi in Guizhou province — which confirmed his supremacy — met up with the Communists in northern Sichuan in 1935. Following political disagreements, Mao's army proceeded northward to its eventual resting place at Yenan in Shaanxi. Zhang Guotao and his men headed west into Xikang (a fatal mistake, as it turned out). But they left behind Communist forces still strong enough to give the local warlords trouble.

In 1937 Chiang moved strong military forces into Sichuan to establish his full authority, and a pitched battle with the local warlords began to look inevitable. But war was averted at the cost of Liu Xiang's independence: he capitulated and handed over command of his troops to Nanking. In July, the 'Marco Polo Bridge incident', contrived by the Japanese, led to full-scale war between China and Japan. This saved Liu Xiang in his dire straits: he regained control of his army. But he succumbed to a long-standing stomach ailment and died on 20 January 1938.

Unable to hold north China against the Japanese, the Nanking government began transferring its various elements to Chongqing, where it remained for the rest of the war with Japan. Liu's army was absorbed. The Communists took Sichuan over in the course of the civil war that followed the defeat of Japan, and in 1950 the province was placed for several years under the control of Deng Xiaoping, soon to be an important leader in the Peking government and the strong-man of post-Mao China.

The wars in Sichuan from the 1911 Revolution until the Second World War resemble a model for the whole warlord period. First independence, then disunity, dictatorship, economic decline, and fighting with bandits, Communists, KMT troops, other warlords, and finally the Japanese. Nowadays the province is accessible by road, by rail, and by air, and local autonomy movements have disappeared. But as short a time ago as 1967, the Communist Party secretary who ruled Sichuan, Li Jingquan, was accused by the Maoists of running it like 'an independent kingdom', and was overthrown by Red Guards. Can the patterns of the past recur in the event of a power struggle which may follow the step-down of elder statesman Deng Xiaoping? If China ever did break up again into provinces and groups of provinces (which seems unlikely), Sichuan might be among the first to assert its autonomy.

4   The Eastern Warlords

Sun Chuanfang and the League of Five Provinces[1]

ALTHOUGH SUN CHUANFANG, the Nanking warlord, is remembered less well nowadays than more colourful figures such as Feng Yuxiang, he none the less deserves close attention. He ruled more people and commanded richer resources than any other warlord. His area was part of the cultural heartland of China and had extensive contacts with the outside world, including as it did the powerful, foreign-administered city of Shanghai with its massive foreign trade and commerce. He united, if only temporarily, as many as five provinces, with access to central China along the Yangzi River. Sun's wars were in some ways reminiscent of those of the Warring States and Three Kingdoms periods of Chinese history and were fought over places that drip with poetic and historical associations. Most important of all, however, were his weakness as a military commander and the poor internal unity of the League of Five Provinces, because these were what enabled Chiang Kaishek and Li Zongren to capture Nanking so soon after the defeat of Wu Peifu at Wuhan in 1926.

Sun was born in Shandong, graduated from the Beiyang Military Academy at Baoding in 1906, and followed the classic pattern of martial training by rounding off his education in Japan. Wu Peifu noticed the young officer during his war with the Anhui Group in 1920 and promoted him to be military governor of Fujian province in south-east China, for-

---

[1] There is no study of Sun Chuanfang in English. His career can be pieced together principally from Tao Zhuyin's study cited above.

merly under the control of the Anhui Group. In 1924, after further meritorious war service on Wu's behalf, he was moved to the richer and less peripheral province of Zhejiang. By 1926 he had expanded his authority to dominate the provinces of Jiangsu, Zhejiang, Fujian, Anhui, and Jiangxi, making his capital at Nanking in Jiangsu. He named the area the League of Five Provinces.

Though Wu Peifu was Sun's patron and 'teacher', the latter was not over-inclined to help him fight the Southerners by attacking their base-province of Guangdong. Wu himself was heavily committed in the north, fighting the army of the Christian General Feng Yuxiang in the mountains around Nankou, near Peking (while Feng betook himself to Outer Mongolia and Moscow to see the Communism he so admired in action). Feng's men had been fighting well, and Wu needed much help if he was to attack the south as well. There were even grounds to fear that Wu's men would mutiny if sent south. Sun, however, just sat in Nanking drinking with his friends and writing poetry — the traditional activities of the Chinese gentleman.

In July 1926, when the southern revolutionary armies were launching the Northern Expedition against the warlords, Sun let it be known that he favoured a national armistice and a peace conference. He proposed the withdrawal of Manchurian and Shandong troops from Peking, which they had occupied earlier in the year. Sun's stated aim was to spare the people of east China the horrors of war, and despite his assurance to Wu, he put it about that he wished to remain neutral in any fight among the other principal warlords. He seemed anxious to avoid war with the Southerners, too, for their armies were well-trained and highly motivated. Early in 1926 Sun actually had secret contacts with Canton, in which it was proposed he should not resist the Northern Expedition at all.

The Southerners' expeditionary army pushed into Hunan in June–July 1926. The local peasantry came to their aid by acting as decoys and positioning tree-trunk-like artillery barrels, while firing their ancient rook-rifles and setting off fire-crackers to undermine the Northerners' morale. They also cut telegraph lines and weakened bridges, and guided the revolutionary soldiers along short-cuts to descend on the enemy with complete surprise.

Sun Chuanfang was afraid that the fighting in Hunan would leave the way open to Chiang Kaishek's armies for an offensive down the Yangzi into the five provinces he controlled, starting with Jiangxi. In this he was right. Indeed Canton had already appointed a 'pacification commissioner' for Jiangsu, a direct threat to Sun's authority.

Sun did nothing to help Wu Peifu's troops resist the Southerners in Hunan, despite the latter's urgent pleas, for he wanted to see the northern and southern armies exhaust each other, leaving him safely in control of east China. He would tell people: 'The Kwangtung [revolutionary] army is like a ball of twine — you can't cut it with a knife. But let it be stretched out, and you can cut it with a pair of scissors.' He doubtless took this view because of his own experience; he had once been able to inflict defeat on the Manchurians and their Shandong allies when they were spread out along the Tientsin–Pukou Railway. But Sun had to keep up an appearance of loyalty to Wu, as his former commander, which inhibited him from trying to snatch the provinces of Hunan and Hubei himself.

His ambitions for a larger league of at least seven provinces could be glimpsed, and had his ambition been realized, the Southerners would have had great difficulty in pursuing the Northern Expedition beyond Hunan. At the same time, Sun was wary of the danger of the Manchurians, led by Zhang Zuolin, grabbing the league provinces of Jiangsu and Zhejiang, on the east China coast, if he were away fighting in central China.

Sun's hold over his commanders, for that matter, was not very secure, and although his forces claimed an overall total of more than 200,000 men, it was doubtful how many of them would back him to the hilt in actual warfare. Nor did he have any great political or reform programme that might have caught people's imagination and increased their loyalty to him. The most satisfactory aspect of his situation in 1926 was his good relationship with Zhang Zongchang, the pro-Manchurian Shandong tyrant, who had given him assurances that if he, Zhang, had to move out to attack Wu Peifu, he would not cross Sun's territory in Jiangsu, but would use the Peking–Hankou Railway to go south and do battle.

Sun Chuanfang now decided the time had come to 'cut the thread' of the so far victorious southerners' communications and supplies, which had been stretched by the unexpected speed with which they had pursued their offensive, astonishing even themselves with their victories. He divided his troops up into five provincial armies and attacked Chiang Kaishek's forces in the middle of their northward march in September 1926. At the same time he sent Chiang a telegram, calling on him to withdraw to Guangdong province within twenty-four hours and restore the government of Hunan to that province's people (a strange contrast with Sun's treatment of the autonomy movement in Zhejiang one month later).

Chiang Kaishek naturally declined to yield, and for the next ten days the two armies were locked in a stalemated battle between the towns of Xinyu and Fenyi, southwest of the Jiangxi capital Nanchang. Revolutionary students and workers in Nanchang, in alliance with the provincial militia, welcomed the Southerners and threw open the city gates in late September. This was a major prize for any army seeking to control the lower Yangtze, even though the city is located some 100 miles south of the great river.

This was an important setback for Sun Chuanfang, who immediately took a river steamer up from Nanking to Jiujiang, a small treaty port, to oversee the fighting. In meetings with the provincial gentry in east China (who mistrusted him because he was from Shandong), Sun boasted that his enemies were 'not worth the name of troops', and vowed to return victorious to Nanking. In October the southern troops evacuated Nanchang — a poor way to repay the revolutionaries there who had welcomed them in. The eastern troops entered Nanchang, closed the gates, and carried out a terrible massacre of supporters of the revolution, while looting to their hearts' content.

The KMT was hampered in its battle with Sun Chuanfang by the fact that part of it strength had been sent to besiege Wu Peifu's forces in the city of Wuchang. (Wuchang was the site of the original revolutionary uprising in 1911.) Besides that, Chiang's command of the offensive in Jiangxi had shown signs of vacillation and his troop commanders were not working well together, each blaming the other for the loss of Nanchang. Now Chiang took firmer hold of the reins. He telegraphed orders to Canton to wind up the sixteen-month-old strike against British-ruled Hong Kong, and had the striking workers armed for service in Jiangxi.

Two of the three components of the triple city of Wuhan, Hanyang, and Hankou, had fallen easily enough to the Southerners. This placed their supplies and arsenals under the control of the KMT forces, which in that battle area were led by leftists and Communists allegedly co-operating with the KMT in the common cause of rooting out the northern warlords. But Wuchang proved a tougher nut, despite the demoralization of its defenders during the forty-one-day siege. The northern troops there numbered about 10,000, though the command was fragmented and ill-co-ordinated. The 100,000 or so inhabitants quickly fell prey to hunger as grain stocks were requisitioned for the troops, and there were problems with water supply as well. More than 2,000 people died of disease. The Wuchang Chamber of Commerce — representing public opinion in the absence of a civil government during the siege — twice asked the besieging southern expeditionary force to let the people leave the city.

The primitive nature of siege warfare during the warlord period is exemplified by the account given by the pro-Communist commander Zhang Guotao, who described a visit he paid to Ye Ting, the famous Cantonese general in charge of the siege of Wuchang.

> The headquarters of his regiment was located at Yonghu, a few *li* south of Wuchang city, and within the range of artillery fire from the city. I lingered at the front for the entire afternoon and stayed overnight at Ye's headquarters. Ye's regiment had only one portable 7.5 centimetre mountain gun. Ye told me that if he used the cannon to shell the city, the enemy would send more shells to the vicinity of the regimental headquarters. The only scouting plane that the Expeditionary Army possessed often flew over the skies of Wuchang. In the city there were several anti-aircraft guns that would fire on the plane, and clouds of black smoke would appear around the plane.

Ye, soon after Zhang's visit, became so downhearted at his casualties that he took himself off to Shanghai, declaring that nobody cared about him or his regiment. Zhang Guotao had to persuade him to make a self-criticism and return to his command.

On 17 September the Southerners' plane dropped propaganda leaflets over the city, urging the troops and citizens to surrender, otherwise they would be shelled with heavy cannon. (Perhaps General Ye had received fresh equipment, or perhaps he was just bluffing.) By now the besiegers had been joined by the KMT's crack Fourth Army, and an assault was planned. On 3–6 October, some 38,000 women and children were permitted to leave the city; they were so eager to get out that some were trampled to death while others fell into the moat and drowned.

The garrison of northern troops was in a defeatist mood, so unwilling to fight that the southern troops used to come to the wall to chat with them and throw up packages of food and cigarettes. Neither Wu Peifu nor Sun Chuanfang could offer the defenders promise of relief, and the Southerners were finally admitted to the city without much fighting on 10 October.

The capture of Wuchang naturally weakened Sun Chuanfang's position on the lower Yangtze; at the same time he faced trouble in his rear, in the rich and independent-minded province of Zhejiang, where the important cities of Hangzhou and Ningbo are located. Zhejiang was ruled by a governor, Xia Chao, who had accumulated strong police and security forces, and who now made a bid for autonomy. He cut the rail link to Shanghai and dispersed the Hangzhou garrison in an attempt to gain full military control of the province. In October 1926, in collusion with other commanders and some civilian political figures, Xia's Zhejiang announced its 'autonomy' and called on its soldiers serving outside the province to return (many did).

Sun Chuanfang, still heavily committed on the Yangtze, stalled for time and pretended to approve the departure of his Zhejiang troops. But he secretly prepared a strike force which suddenly fell on Xia's rebels at night. Xia was shot in a firefight while trying to escape, and many of his men were machine-gunned out of hand. Xia's head was exhibited on a spike as a warning to others.

However, Zhejiang was still not 'pacified'. Sun dispatched one of his senior Zhejiang-born commanders, Chen Yi,[2] to assume control of the province. But Chen took him too literally, for on arriving in Hangzhou, he convened a meeting of provincial public figures to discuss a proclamation of independence. Sun was far from conceding the wealthy coastal province. He reshuffled his remaining divisions to place them in positions from which they could easily invade Zhejiang. During this process Sun had to keep a wary eye on Wu Peifu, who, having seen his men surrender at Wuchang, would doubtless have relished the chance of occupying Zhejiang, which would have given him the chance to attack

[2] This is not the same Chen Yi who was a famous Communist commander in the civil war and later became foreign minister of the People's Republic.

the KMT's rear and flank. The KMT, however, stirred the pot by proclaiming support for Chen Yi and appointing him commander of its Nineteenth Army.

The Hangzhou meeting acclaimed Chen and eight other local men and called on them to form a committee to plan the province's political future. Their first act was to send telegrams to Sun Chuanfang in Nanking and to Chiang Kaishek, who was fighting on the Yangzi, asking them to withdraw whatever military forces they had in Zhejiang. Their dream, it seems, was to create a third force in Chinese politics and put an end to the division of the country into north and south.

Meanwhile Sun held an emergency meeting with Shandong's tyrannical *dujun* Zhang Zongchang, and other powerful warlords, to decide how to keep the KMT armies from capturing the cities of the lower Yangtze, from where they could overrun Shandong and strike at Peking. Zhang, an ally of the Manchurians, suggested that he ship his men by sea to 'defend' Shanghai and the Jiangsu coastline; but Sun was too cautious to permit that. He decided, to liquidate the new provincial 'government' in Zhejiang. On 24 October at four o'clock in the morning his men poured into Hangzhou and immediately disarmed the police and provincial garrison. This put an end to Hangzhou's short-lived bid for autonomy, and underlined Sun's warning that only military strength could guarantee the independence of any province.

After Sun's troops had recaptured Nanchang and taken up defensive positions along the Yangtze, he worked out plans to drive the Southerners out of the centrally-located provinces of Jiangxi, Hunan, and Hubei. The fall of Wuchang put this plan in doubt, but Sun was hoping that warlord forces from the westerly province of Sichuan, on the upper Yangtze, would move down-river and attack the triple city of Wuhan. The Southerners were not idle, either: two Hunanese armies had mauled Sun's troops badly in different parts of Jiangxi.

Sun came up-river from Nanking by steamer, preparing to launch another offensive against the southern occupation forces at Wuhan. But as he approached Jiujiang, he found the situation had deteriorated so badly that he secretly transferred to another steamer and sailed downstream again. The situation in Jiujiang was one which always made a warlord nervous: marines from Japanese, British, and American gunboats had been landed to protect the foreign concessions in the town, and there was a danger of large-scale foreign intervention if fighting broke out.

With this, Sun's Jiangxi forces began to fall apart, and on 6 November the KMT army occupied Jiujiang. Sun's principal division commanders fell back on Nanking and Hangzhou. Others held positions at Anqing and Wuhu and around Lake Tai. The 'League of Five Provinces' disintegrated, and Wuhan was saved for the Southerners.

When they took Nanchang for the second time, in November, the KMT handed Sun's commanders over to the masses, who stuck placards on their necks and denounced them for 'waging war and beggaring the people'. After the massacres and looting they had perpetrated, they could expect no mercy. They were paraded around the city in open chairs for everyone to see. Five of them were tried and shot.

Meanwhile, in Sun Chuanfang's rear, the situation was quickly getting out of hand. Pro-Communist Shanghai workers staged an uprising, and armed bands roamed the streets, firing on policemen. But the rebellion was quickly put down. The foreign concessions in Shanghai were defended by troops and warships of the various nations represented, so that no warlord forces or armed rebels could enter them. But in the chanceries of Tokyo, London, and Washington, alarm was mounting about the safety of foreign civilians in China. Intervention was favoured by the British, but the Japanese cautioned against it.

Sun Chuanfang declared all the new political bodies illegal, closed down the Shanghai General Trade Union, and proscribed the city's United Congress of Workers and

Students. Li Baozhang, the notoriously brutal commander of the Shanghai garrison, began savage retaliatory measures against workers, students, party members, and those whom the leftists liked to call 'democratic and progressive figures'. The Chinese-ruled parts of Shanghai were subjected to a wave of 'white terror'.

The foreign community in Shanghai was opposed to the entry into the city of any warlord's troops. In 1925 and again in 1927 the International Settlement police force, backed up by troops from the concessionary powers, disarmed and interned warlord soldiers who crossed its lines in flight or in search of sanctuary.

In February–March 1927, the International Council which ran the settlement (dominated by the British) addressed a letter to the various foreign consuls concerning the danger of 'the impending arrival in this neighbourhood of large bodies of Chinese troops belonging to the armies now engaged in the civil war in the country'. The council also mobilized the Shanghai Volunteer Force, an international military unit set up in 1903, comprising about a thousand men including light horse, field artillery, four 4.5 inch howitzers, ten armoured cars each with one .303 Vickers machine-gun, and an American mounted unit with two motorized Lewis guns. The composition of the infantry force was on national lines, with two companies of British volunteers, as well as companies made up of Japanese, Chinese, Russians, Portuguese, and 'Shanghai Scottish'. They paraded and drilled once a fortnight and were inspected annually by the British general officer commanding troops in China.

Although Chinese revolutionaries often denounced the domination by foreigners of this city on Chinese soil, it served them well as a sanctuary when the going got tough under the jurisdiction of the KMT or the warlords. Many of China's noted revolutionaries and left-wing intellectuals in the 1920s and 1930s took advantage of the lax political and social atmosphere and the free intellectual climate in Shanghai before the Japanese occupation. On several occasions the KMT authorities, after their victory in east China, tried to order the Shanghai courts to hand over Communists sheltering in the International Settlement. Judges in the settlement's courts often knocked back such requests.

While the southern expeditionary army was fighting its way down the Yangtze in November 1926, the northern warlords were showing alarm at the speed of its advance and the loss of Wuhan. The menace was heightened by the fact that Feng Yuxiang, the Christian general, in yet another of his mercurial changes of course, showed signs of preparing to help the Southerners against the warlords. His army, equipped with Soviet munitions, was moving on central China through the north-western province of Shaanxi, having extricated itself from the positions at Nankou near Peking where Marshal Wu Peifu had tried to destroy it.

The Shandong *dujun* Zhang Zongchang, fearing defeat if Feng joined up with the KMT's expeditionary forces, convened a conference of the main northern commanders and their representatives. Neither Sun Chuanfang nor Marshal Wu Peifu — both still considered to be allies — was represented, however. Zhang Zuolin, the Manchurian leader, opened the proceedings by declaring that he had no ambitions to become president of China (as people suspected) and that he wished mainly to discuss military matters. Marshals Sun and Wu, he said, should be consulted about the deliberations, and there should also be overtures to the Shanxi *dujun*, Yan Xishan. (Yan shortly afterwards joined forces with the expeditionary army from the south.)

The meeting decided that Shandong and the military forces in Zhili should 'aid' Jiangsu (that is, Sun Chuanfang). The Manchurians would 'aid' their old arch-enemy, Wu Peifu, who was still in Zhengzhou, the capital of Henan, licking the wounds he had received at Wuhan. He was to be asked by Zhang Zuolin to join the Manchurians in a campaign to 'aid' Shaanxi, and resist Feng Yuxiang's advance from that quarter.

Whenever warlords got together to talk about 'aiding' one of their counterparts who was in difficulties, everyone knew that what they really sought was an easy means of carving up the other's territory and absorbing his troops and munitions into their own armies. So the sincerity of the Tientsin meeting in discussing 'aid' for Marshals Wu and Sun was a sensitive matter and difficult to substantiate, especially as they were not present.

The meeting decided that Marshal Wu should be asked to withdraw from the Peking–Hankou Railway (his most important line of north–south communications), and let the Manchurians try their hand at a fight with the KMT and Communist-led armies at Wuhan. Meanwhile Sun Chuanfang should be asked to attempt another offensive up the Yangtze to regain Jiujiang and Nanchang. The Zhili and Shandong troops would guard the Tientsin–Pukou Railway, which was the main line of communication from the north into Jiangsu.

This was the closest the northern warlords ever got to uniting in sincere co-operation to fight the south's expeditionary force. Had they been able to effect such co-operation in practice, they could well have beaten Generalissimo Chiang Kaishek and his armies, and the Chinese revolution would have been set back by years, if not by decades. But unity was something the warlords could never attain; they were too interested in settling old scores and taking short-term advantage of each other's weaknesses or defeats. With five major armies vying for control of north China, the Southerners could divide and rule even though their own unity was less than perfect.

On 19 November, a guard brought in a name-card and gave it to Zhang Zuolin during a session of the Tientsin conference. He jumped up and shouted: 'Is it really him? Ask him in immediately!' A square-faced man, with one ear bigger than the other, entered the conference chamber. Most of the other delegates had never met him before, so there were hasty introductions, whereupon Sun Chuanfang — for it was he — joined the meeting and metaphorically laid his cards on the table. 'We wheat-eating northerners,' he said, 'will never get on with those rice-eating Southerners.'

In this way the Shandong-born Sun reasserted his northern origins and humbly explained that he no longer felt up to defending Jiangsu. The Shandong commanders, if they wished, could transfer their headquarters to Nanking, the capital of Jiangsu, while he himself would be content to fall back on Zhejiang (regardless of his unpopularity there).

Manchuria's Zhang Zuolin, despite his pleasure at this unexpected windfall from a warlord previously considered hostile, now had to turn his attention to the ticklish subject of Marshal Wu Peifu, until now regarded as Sun's mentor and ally. Although Wu's military performance in recent years had been less than brilliant, he still commanded much prestige. As he had not attended the meeting in Tientsin, it had been impossible to assign him a role in the projected new alliance. He was known to be touchy, and would be a great nuisance if he felt himself slighted by the conference's decisions. So Zhang Zuolin merely invited him, an 'elder brother and ally' to visit Tientsin for consultations, and himself refrained from accepting the title of grand marshal (commander-in-chief) or president of the Republic — posts which were at that time vacant.

Zhang Zuolin sent a representative to Wu in Zhengzhou, asking him whether he was proposing to counter-attack the KMT and pro-Communist forces at Wuhan–and if not, would he kindly let the Manchurians attack them after passing through his lines on the Peking–Hankou Railway. Alternatively, would he like to come to Peking with a high-sounding title and do staff work?

Wu, anxious to keep the Manchurians out of the central China province of Henan, where he now had his base, suggested in a telegram to Zhang Zuolin that the latter should take his armies south by sea and attack the home province of the KMT, Guangdong. The two men played telegraphic cat-and-mouse with each other, the argument eventually coming down to that most useful of warlord excuses for doing nothing — shortage of supplies.

Rebuffed by Wu, Zhang at last decided to assume the title of grand marshal, and began inviting the Peking diplomatic corps to official receptions and tea-parties. But he met with a cool reception from most of the ministers, who were consulting their respective governments about whether to recognize the new regime.

Meanwhile Chiang Kaishek's armies had successfully pushed down the Yangtze, with Sun's men retreating before them. In Shanghai the foreign population, though defended by 10,000 regular troops of their various nationalities — not to mention the gallant volunteers — grew anxious about the advance of the KMT army early in 1927. Sun Chuanfang seemed on the brink of involving the Powers in a fight with the approaching Southerners. The various foreign concessions arrested people they thought might be Communist agents and, contrary to later practice, handed them over to the ill mercy of Sun's police, without referring them to the courts of the International Settlement. The Communists resisted with assassination of public figures and the calling of a general strike. Sun's garrison retaliated with summary beheadings in the streets.

Dissension between the KMT and the Communists at Wuhan grew during the spring of 1927. Sun could have played on this split more than he did. Instead he saw his position deteriorate when a division of his troops defected with its commander to the KMT forces on the borders of Anhui province. Foreigners living along the Yangtze were intimidated by the advance of the KMT troops, whom they referred to collectively as 'Cantonese', and tended to regard as Communists. Memories of previous anti-foreign pogroms sent many merchants and missionaries fleeing down-river to Shanghai.

Sun and his new Shandong ally Zhang Zongchang ordered their troops to withdraw from the Shanghai area to defend Nanking, which lay up-river and was in Chiang Kaishek's path. In March another southern army advanced northwards from the area of Lake Tai, while the main force side-stepped

Sun's riverine defenses and headed for Nanking from the south. Some expeditionary forces entered the Chinese area of Shanghai and routed the remnants of Sun's army in desperate fighting which raged around, but did not spill into, the International Settlement. Chiang had reassuring messages sent to the foreign communities who, however, reinforced their garrison from troopships. Foreign warships took up stations off-shore, ready to shell any Chinese troops who threatened the Concessions.

Late in March 1927, the Southerners under Chiang Kaishek entered Nanking, and the troops killed and injured a number of foreigners, while others escaped only by climbing down a rope slung from the top of the old city wall. British and Japanese gunboats shelled the city in retaliation, and the incident grated still more on the fears of foreigners in Shanghai and other places. It damaged Chiang's prospects of improving relations with the Powers, which anyway preferred the warlord Sun to the 'Bolshevik' Chiang. It would not be long before they saw their estimation of Chiang's politics contradicted.

Sun Chuanfang and Zhang Zongchang retreated north of the Yangtze to block Chiang Kaishek from invading Shandong. Some southern units crossed the river and occupied towns on its north bank. In August, Sun counterattacked with three columns totalling 50,000 to 60,000 men. So deficient was the KMT's military intelligence that it was only by chance that three southern generals were sailing down the Yangtze on a gunboat towards Nanking when they came across a large body of men being ferried across the river. Their uniforms were not those of southern troops, and after receiving no reply to their challenge, the KMT generals ordered their gunboat to open fire. The troops attempting to cross to the south bank replied with rifle and machine-gun fire. More than ten boats were sunk and many men killed or drowned. Some men on the gunboat were wounded, too. The survivors of the northern force escaped down-river.

However, the fortunes of war were not all for the south. When all the expedition's forces which had succeeded in crossing the river had been driven back across the Yangtze to its right (south) bank, Sun Chuanfang saw the Southerners' positions crumble along the lower stretch, partly due to the Northerners' superiority in artillery. In addition, there was friction between the troops from Wuhan and Chiang Kaishek's men, so co-operation among their commanders was poor. Sun could see a crucial turning-point in the battle to recover his lost territory, including Nanking and Shanghai.

Zhang Zuolin's Manchurian and Zhang Zongchang's Shandong army were not in a mood to cross the Yangtze again and fight a stiff battle on the other shore. So they agreed that Sun should have a free hand. The expeditionary troops now made hasty preparation for renewed battle. The First and Seventh armies hurried down-river to oppose the Northerners' crossings. With a pincer movement they caught one of the northern columns at Longtan, near Nanking, and soon the river was full of floating corpses.

The Guangxi commander Bai Chongxi hurried reinforcements up from Shanghai, and Sun's invasion force was soon backed up against the river and fighting for its life. Sun and about a thousand of his men escaped to the northern shore on an old steamer. He urgently requested Zhang Zongchang to fortify the garrisons there, but Zhang made the excuse that he could not spare any men from the confrontation with Feng Yuxiang's 'Christian' army in east Henan, which threatened to invade Shandong. So in early September, Sun had to abandon Pukou, Yangzhou, and other garrisoned cities on the north bank.

The Southerners confiscated the weapons of the captured or killed Northerners, and shot one of their own commanders for having skulked in Shanghai when he should have been pursuing the enemy. The northern warlords had failed in their last big counter-attack, and the path to Peking was now clearly marked for Chiang Kaishek.

Sun continued to hold commands in the 'National Pacification Army' until June 1928, when Marshal Zhang Zuolin was assassinated by the Japanese, and General Zhang Zongchang was forced by their military encroachment to flee Shandong.

Sun Chuanfang escaped to Japanese-held Dairen (Dalian) in Manchuria, and was later assassinated by the daughter of one of his officers whose execution he had ordered. If there was any moral to his brief career as a major warlord, it was that technology had rendered irrelevant many of the strategic rules of civil war in traditional China. The same geographical constraints applied, but they were easier to overcome. Railways, modern artillery, the telegraph, repeating rifles, and other innovations had telescoped the old pattern of warfare to such an extent that victories previously involving years of manoeuvring could now be brought off in a few months or weeks. The imposing, leisurely progress of princely armies across the landscape was replaced by confused and disorganized scurrying through smoke and shrapnel, in cattle-trucks or with baggage carried by mule, dodging the occasional, haphazard rain of shells. China was absorbing the principles of modern warfare — the anonymous killing of often unseen enemies, the inflicting of wounds worse than any previously witnessed, high explosives, and the elimination of chivalry and codes of military honour, which in past ages had captured the thrilled imagination of schoolboys and even scholars. The five provinces became the bastion of Kuomintang power and remained so until the Japanese invasion.

Zhang Zongchang

The popular image of a warlord — ruthless, cruel, avaricious, and addicted to vice — cannot be applied totally to most of the actual military leaders of the period. We have found traits of dualism and personal frugality among several important warlords, although in each of them there was pride, hot temper, and, by modern standards, indifference to the sufferings of their own soldiers and of the common people whose labour and produce they lived off. However, in the dictator of Shandong province — the feared and reviled General Zhang Zongchang — all the worst traits of his class were present, with barely a redeeming feature.

Shandong is the most easterly of China's provinces, and historically one of the most significant. A wedge-shape promontory with an area roughly equivalent to that of New Zealand, it is the native land of Confucius — in his day known as the Kingdom of Lu — and it was here that the sage evolved and tested his theories of society and government in the sixth and fifth centuries BC. The province has a temperate climate, and the chief crops nowadays are maize and wheat, though rice, millet, sorghum, and sweet potato are also grown and silk is an important industry. The landscape is reminiscent of the hillier parts of Europe. Houses are solidly built with local stone or grey fired brick, with distinctive decorations on the tiled roofs. The Yellow River, traditionally the main artery of China's ancient culture, empties itself through Shandong into the Gulf of Bohai, though it has changed its course drastically several times.

To the north-west, Shandong's borders match with those of Hebei — called Zhili during the warlord period — and to the west with Henan. In the south it borders on Anhui and Jiangsu; its northern edge is coastal, and its eastward tip points towards Korea. Parts of the province are mountainous.

The people of Shandong have historically been noted for their independence and strong physique. They have been sought after as soldiers and policemen, even as far afield as Hong Kong. China's most famous historical novel about armed rebellion — variously translated as *The Water Margin, Outlaws of the Marsh*, and *All Men are Brothers* — is set in Shandong.

The province's long coastline has made it vulnerable to piracy and encroachment by foreign navies. From the 1890s until the First World War, the Germans and Japanese vied for control of the valuable peninsula. Qingdao, the principal port, was built almost entirely by the Germans (using local labour, of course). It ranks with Shanghai and Tientsin as one of the most foreign-looking cities in China. Britain also had interests in Shandong during the period of foreign dominance: she demanded and obtained a lease on the port of Weihaiwei, handing it back to China only in 1930.

Japan had been nominally allied to the British and French against Germany in the First World War and in 1914 seized Qingdao from the Germans after a fierce battle, occupying in addition the railway to Jinan, the provincial capital. At the Versailles peace conference in 1919, Japan's interests in Shandong were recognized by the other powers, touching off a furore of nationalist sentiment in China and pushing that country faster along the road to genuine revolution than would otherwise have been the case.

Zhang Zongchang, who ruled Shandong despotically from 1925 until 1928, was little more than a street urchin born in Yi county. In 1911 he joined a bandit gang and was seen to be both strong and courageous. The bandits ended up by joining the forces of the warlord of Jiangsu province, and Zhang rose quickly in his commands. Through assassination and the fortunes of war, he attracted the attention of one of the vice-presidents of the ineffectual northern Republican government and was given high military posts.

Zhang, like most Chinese of his day and even nowadays, was intensely superstitious and fell (like Liu Xiang in Sichuan) under the influence of a Daoist soothsayer. The prophesier correctly predicted that on a particular day a train full of enemy troops would be derailed — which it was, for the soothsayer had allegedly bribed some peasants to remove the rail-bolts.

Appointed military governor of Shandong in 1925, Zhang made it his hobby to split the heads of executed persons in two, or to hang them from telephone poles, as though they were listening to the wires. While he made several military excursions to fight other warlords, Zhang was always careful to keep the rich and secure province of Shandong at his back, retiring there to recuperate. He imposed innumerable taxes on the local people — taxes on rice, tobacco, firewood, dogs, rickshaws, livestock, brothels, and so on. He collected 'donations' for a shrine and bronze statue of himself. He issued near-worthless paper money and forced people to accept it. He extorted money from banks, and misappropriated his soldiers' wages. He made opium his regime's monopoly.

Zhang was semi-literate — when asked which university he graduated from he would say: 'The College of the Green Forest' (that is, banditry). He was variously nicknamed Dog-Meat General and Lanky General. He was physically un-attractive, with a bullet-head and cruel, curling lips, and on top of that was well over six feet tall. He kept extensive harems of Chinese, Russian, Japanese, and European women, with whom he spent much time when not fighting. His own favourite sobriquet was 'Great General of Justice and Might'.

Some of the most vivid reminiscences of Zhang Zong-chang's life-style were given by Frank Sutton. Sutton was sent by Zhang Zuolin on a tour of inspection in Shandong (Zhang Zongchang regarded the Manchurian Zhang as his ally and patron). Arriving at the Grand Hotel in Peking, Sutton and a travelling companion enquired about rooms. The manager told them none could be had — 'until his Excellency leaves'. Hearing the strains of 'Alexander's Ragtime Band' coming from the ballroom, they made their way there, to find a somewhat listless dance in progress.

> In the centre and occupying a whole sofa lounged a
> monstrous figure in sky-blue uniform resplendent with
> gold lace, but partly obscured by an extremely pretty
> golden-haired girl in a scanty gown and dripping with
> diamonds, who occupied his lap.[3]

There was a hush as Sutton strode into the room. Zhang
Zongchang rose to meet him — and struck him a vigorous
blow in the chest. Sutton returned the compliment with his
sole fist: they guffawed and embraced. What business they
subsequently transacted is not recorded, but in 1924 Sutton
was again sent by Zhang Zuolin to Shandong to inspect some
batteries of field artillery which had been deposited there by
his Manchurian troops. Sutton found the guns in shocking
condition — rusted and with parts missing. He allowed them
to be fired for a demonstration in front of Zhang Zongchang,
and predictably some of them misfired or blew up. The warlord was furious and threatened to execute any officer who
ordered the firing of a gun in such bad condition. Next day
Sutton had to witness the beheading of one such wretch: he
was tipped skilfully from a rickshaw with his hands bound,
and his head expertly lopped off, the neck arteries spouting
blood before the corpse even hit the ground.

Zhang Zongchang's crack troops were former Russian
imperial army officers who had fled the revolution and
sought service with whomsoever would employ them. They
were typical of their breed, totally careless of personal danger, violent, drunken, and sentimental. But they knew about
modern warfare and seemed disinclined to seek any other
form of employment, as long as they could get alcohol and,
occasionally, women.

An impressive description of the Russian officers has
been left by A. Krarup-Nielsen, a Danish writer who visited
China in 1927. Arriving via south China at the area of the
most recent front, he did the proper thing for a European
visitor by betaking himself to the Tientsin Club, where the

---

[3] Charles Drage, *Soldier of Fortune*, London: Heinemann, 1963, p. 176.

nationals of eight concession-holding countries sought their ease over billiards and Scotch. There he fell in with the American military attaché, a giant of a man, and the correspondent (unnamed) of the *North China Daily News*, one of the leading English-language newspapers in China at the time.

Their first, albeit indirect contact with General Zhang Zongchang was the sight on a freight train of a resplendent new motor car, said to belong to his number four concubine. The trains were otherwise very crowded with soldiers. Everywhere the three Westerners went, the Chinese troops called out to them for *papirosy* (Russian cigarettes with a hollow cardboard tube at one end). When the train arrived at Yanzhou, a rail junction in south western Shandong, they were delighted to be refreshed with Pilsener beer by a white-bearded German bishop, and next day pressed on towards the war zone.

At Tengxian, near the borders of Jiangsu province, they ran into the spearhead of the coming attack by the Shandong men on Nationalist troops and the forces of Feng Yuxiang. Here they discovered the importance of that most familiar weapon platform and troop transport of the Russian civil war — the armoured train.

Skilful use of such trains by Leon Trotsky and other Soviet military leaders in Russia had led to the final defeat of the Tsarist armies and the expulsion of the Allied intervention force. Now they had become the spearhead of the northern warlords' fighting forces wherever, that is, the tracks were in good repair and there was fuel to be had. On the other hand, the trains were highly limited as regards manoeuvrability and were very vulnerable to shelling (see plate 22).

Three trains in all were to lead the Shandong assault on the Nationalist and 'Christian' forces. The American attaché returned to Peking, but the Dane and his newsman companion found lodgings with a Roman Catholic priest — who at first refused to admit them because he thought they were Russians.

A tremendous racket of small-arms and machine-gun fire awoke them in the night, but it turned out to be an attack by bandits, which the city garrison beat off, though they lost their commanding officer. Krarup-Nielsen noticed, in passing, the inferiority of the Shandong and other northern soldiers to the KMT Southerners — 'in discipline, organisation, training, military carriage and fighting spirit'.

With the arrival of the armoured train *Shandong* (the trains were christened like ships), the travellers squeezed aboard amidst the Russian officers, who instantly invited them to share their black bread and cabbage soup, to say nothing of a bottle of cognac ordered by a French-speaking officer. They learned that General Zhang had promised the Russians a reward of 300,000 Mexican dollars if they could capture the beautiful, Venice-like city of Suzhou in Jiangsu province, where the KMT had their headquarters for the time being.

This exemplified the tremendous increase in the mobility of Chinese troops by comparison with that of a mere three decades earlier. The railways, few and far between though they were by European standards, followed in the main the natural routes used for centuries by people riding on horseback, on mules, in sedan chairs, or just marching from one province to another. If the tracks were clear, the Russian-led armies from Shandong could reach Suzhou in a day and a night, but resistance was to be expected, and the signalling and shunting facilities were less than satisfactory in the midst of a civil war.

Control of railheads and junctions had become a vital factor in Chinese warfare, transforming it almost as much as the machine-gun had done in the West during the First World War. The Danish writer called trains 'the very backbone — military as well as moral — of the whole Chinese army on taking the field.' But that, of course, was because military aviation was till in its infancy.

The *Shandong* and its companions *Henan* and *Peking* were constructed along identical lines. Krarup-Nielsen writes:

All three armoured trains had been constructed on the same system. The front and rear wagons were long, flat, open goods trucks, destined for carrying spare parts of machinery and rails, tools, etc; also meant as a sort of buffer to break the impact should mines be encountered on the line, placed there by the enemy's engineers. Next followed, at each end of the train, a strong armoured truck fitted with heavy guns in circular, revolving turrets as on a man-of-war; also a number of machine-guns showing their teeth through the crevices between the armoured plates covering the sides of the truck.

Then came a second armoured truck at each end, doing duty as tumbrels, and likewise armed with machine-guns. Finally, the engine itself, in front of a square plate box, like a case. Right in the middle of the train was found the armoured wagon which served as the eating, sleeping and recreation space for the Russian officers whenever they had a few moments off between the onslaughts. Most of them, however, were so taken up with watching the effect of the cannonade during an attack that they preferred getting up on to the roof of their wagon instead of sheltering inside, or standing beside the trains to watch developments through their field-glasses. There was a telephone connection between the officers' wagon, the armoured trucks and the engine. As the crew numbered about eighty there was very little room to spare, each cubic inch being accurately calculated.[4]

With a long blast on its whistle, the *Shandong* moved off to war, followed by its two comrades. For most of the morning, no sign of the enemy was reported. Then there was an abrupt halt to replace a bolt which had been removed from the rails by the enemy; the repairs were easily carried out but could have derailed the train had it been night-time and the sabotage gone unnoticed. Suddenly the *Shandong* came under fire

[4] A. Krarup-Nielsen, *The Dragon Awakes*, London: The Bodley Head, 1928, p. 163.

from an enemy train up the line; the Chinese repair gangs worked on with no sign of fear.

During the night the *Shandong* came under fire again from an enemy train. A few Russians and Shandong soldiers were wounded, whereupon the embattled train loosed off a furious hail of return fire. Then the news came that infantrymen up the line had defeated the troops of Chiang Kaishek and Feng Yuxiang, and blocked their advance on Peking. The Nationalists had suffered a serious defeat, and their three armoured trains were captured.

Medical facilities for the wounded were atrocious. Krarup-Nielsen wrote:

> The Chinese military authorities were sublimely indifferent to the matter; they did not even provide drinking water for the wounded. Those who were able to crawl out of the wagons at the stopping places, or at least push forward until they reached the doors, were sometimes able to get hold of some eatables of a sort from the village people coming to the stations on purpose to traffic with soldiers.
>
> If what I heard was true, that the Chinese soldiers were apt to be very harsh in their treatment of the country people when marching through their villages, I can testify that the village women, on their side, made them pay exorbitant prices for each drink of water, each green cucumber or slice of water-melon bought.
>
> The most severely wounded, unable to fight for themselves, were entirely forgotten on such occasions. It was a rare sight to see any of their comrades help them to a drink of water or the like. When one saw a circle of comrades standing round a dying soldier it was simply for the sake of laughing at some queer muscular contortion of his limbs, or some other result of his smashed-up condition of agony. Those who died on the way were allowed to lie where they were till we reached our final destination.[5]

[5] Krarup-Nielsen, *The Dragon Awakes*, p. 186.

The Dane was particularly incensed to find Chinese medics lying on stretchers and smoking opium, and threatened to report them to the commanding officer.

The use of trains for military purposes did nothing to improve the service for the civilian passenger. An English-language magazine reported:

> 'It is not only that the commanders are constantly moving troops and delaying traffic; the greatest annoyance is the constant use of any and every train by the common riff-raff of the so-called army who camp in the dining cars and in the first and second class coaches, monopolise all comforts without even paying their fare, and make comfort and sanitation impossible by their filthy and destructive habits. ... On the platform there appears a beplumed and gilded general who announces that he wishes to have a conversation with some other general or politician of standing on board the train. Everything is held up accordingly. The talkative general and his friend ensconce themselves in a first class compartment and absorb tea and political gossip for two or three hours while a ragged squad of coolie soldiers, under a coolie officer, guard the engine and the station master's office and see that no attempt is made to move the train. About the time then that a start is made fifty or a hundred bandoliered ruffians of the local army, who are moved to ride somewhere on an excursion, clamber into the dining-car, sprawl over the table, stack their rifles in the aisles and proceed to spit upon every square inch of floor and wall space that is within range.[6]

Despite his appalling misdeeds, General Zhang Zongchang cut quite a figure socially. Madame Wellington Koo — wife of the Chinese foreign minister at the time — considered herself one of his special favourites when he came calling in Peking. She wrote in her autobiography, *No Feast Lasts Forever*:

[6] *Far Eastern Review*, April 1918.

All warlords at that time reeked of money, but Chang
Tsung-ch'ang [Zhang Zongchang] was so delightfully
outrageous that he was disarming. There were many
stories about him. One was that he had 'the physique of
an elephant, the brain of a pig, and the temperament of
a tiger.' He was said to be 'dangerous even to look at'. He
was also called 'Old Eighty-Six', and the stories about
the nickname varied. Some said he was the height of a
pile of eighty-six silver dollars (impossible, for each dollar would have had to be nearly one inch thick); others
said that figure represented the length of a certain por-
tion of his anatomy. A teakwood coffin always accompanied him in his wars. And he was known everywhere
as the 'Three Don't Knows'. He said he didn't know how
much money he had, how many concubines, or how
many men in his army.

I played poker with him and other minor warlords at
stakes that now make me dizzy. But I didn't try to com-
pete with them. Sometimes one would lose from
$30,000 to $50,000 at a sitting. When the debts were
paid in silver dollars, the players would take their win-
nings home in bags.... Zhang, outrageous as he was in
many ways, recognized my dignity and tried to live up
to my standards. Whenever I went there, he would have
the most expensive food, bird's-nest soup and sharks'
fins, and use his famous $50,000 Belgian cut-glass din-
nerware. Of course, I always took my two favourite
Pekes when I visited him — my Pao Pei and his wife, a
beautiful little stupid chow dog my old friend Sir Hugh
Cunliffe-Owen had managed to send me from England.
Zhang used to roar at the servants: 'Never mind what
you give Madame Koo to eat. But be sure her dogs get
the very best or you'll suffer for it.'

He was ridiculous, of course. But there was a certain
swashbuckling courage about him. In the end he, too,
died violently. When things got bad he came to my husband and asked Wellington to get him a passport so that
he could leave China. Wellington did. But Zhang was
shot in the railroad station. I felt sad when I heard the
news, but it was better that way. He started off as a

wharf coolie and never looked back. I can't imagine him
leading a life of quiet retirement.[7]

A less appealing picture of Zhang is implicit in the description of the poor in Shandong given by General Joseph W.
Stilwell, who visited the area when serving as a young military attaché at the US Legation in Peking. Dead and dying
people littered the streets. The only thing left to eat was
crushed soya-bean cake usually fed to pigs. The peasants'
children were abandoned, their carts and animals seized by
the troops, houses pulled down for firewood — the eternal
misery of poverty in China. Zhang's heavy taxation was
largely to blame for the famine, and even his soldiers ate little more than rice and steamed bread. The general's
armoured trains went to battle so overcrowded with troops
that not a few fell under the wheels on the way after trying
to cling to precarious perches on the outside of the wagons.
The stylishly dressed Russian cavalry in Zhang's employ looted every village they passed through.[8]

Hallett Abend, the correspondent of the *New York Times*,
described a famine in Shandong in 1928. More than 28,000
refugees flooded into Jinan, the provincial capital.

> They camped in the ravines and gullies near the city —
> camped in little pup tents made of woven straw, and
> slept on the bare ground despite the cold winds which
> brought alternate snow squalls and drenching showers.
> Once each day each of these 28,000 wretches was given
> one bowl of hot millet gruel, salted but made without
> the addition of meat or vegetables. Marshal Chang
> Tsung-ch'ang [Zhang Zongchang] was then governor of
> Shantung [Shandong] province, which numbered at
> that time a population of nearly 30,000,000 people.
> And even while the 28,000 people shivered in rags at

[7] Madame Wellington Koo (with Isabella Taves), *No Feast Lasts Forever*,
New York: Quadrangle, 1975, pp. 158–9.

[8] Barbara W. Tuchman, *Stilwell and the American Experience in China
1911–45*, New York: Macmillan, 1971, p. 110.

the gates of his capital, Chang Tsung-ch'ang was host at a great banquet, given in celebration of the installation of a $50,000 central heating system in his spacious yamen.[9]

When Chiang Kaishek massacred the communist workers and students in Shanghai, Zhang's subordinates lent a willing hand, roaming the streets with broadswords and executing anyone who looked suspicious to them. But the swashbuckling general could not forever escape the retribution which is due to men of violence and cruelty. At the urging of Britain and the United States, the Japanese agreed to remove from Shandong the troops which they had stationed there after expelling the Germans in 1914. However, they left behind a sizeable number of Japanese civilians — mostly shopkeepers and small business people — whose presence they considered to justify Japan's continuing to take an active interest in the affairs of the province. In 1928 the Nationalists in their drive on Peking attacked and vanquished the armies of Zhang Zongchang and Sun Chuanfang. On the pretext that the safety of Japanese civilians was jeopardized by the military situation, Japan sent an expeditionary force of 5,000 men to Qingdao and thence up the railway to Jinan, which they damaged heavily with the loss of thousands of Chinese lives. With this new element in the war, Zhang's armies melted away, reduced to little more than roving bands. Zhang threw himself on the mercy of the Nationalist government and begged permission to leave the country. This was granted, but Zhang shortly after was assassinated by a student avenging a wrong done to his father by the 'Great General of Justice and Might'.

---

[9] Hallett Abend, *My Life in China 1926–1941*, New York: Harcourt Brace, 1943, pp. 63–4.

5   The Bandit Way

Not many bandits wrote their memoirs, but by good fortune an intimate view of their hard and dangerous life has survived in the form of a book published in 1926 by Dr Harvey J. Howard, an American ophthalmologist at Peking Union Medical College.[1] Howard was visiting the ranch of his friend Major William Morgan Palmer in northern Manchuria when word came that bandits were harassing a nearby village. They set off to make a show of force and frighten the bandits off. But suddenly the bandits charged them over the brow of a hill, and Palmer, after getting off a few rounds, was shot and killed. Howard was taken prisoner, together with a Chinese boy, Liao.

The bandits were apparently chagrined to learn they had killed Major Palmer, for he was well known in the area and his death might bring retribution. But the first priority of the bandits was to relieve both the living and the dead of all their valuables. Dr Howard wrote:

> One by one the bandits came in to display before me their new possessions. One was wearing Liao's new foreign shoes. Another had put on Major Palmer's shoes and leather puttees. The wearers looked down at their footwear with great admiration, and declared that they were extra fine. A dark-faced, young bandit came in to ask me how my wrist watch should be wound. A fourth showed me how well my Scottish Rite ring looked upon one of his fingers.

Then the bandits interrogated Dr Howard to discover whether he were wealthy and seemed satisfied when he

[1] Harvey J. Howard, *Ten Weeks with Chinese Bandits*, London: John Lane/The Bodley Head, 1926.

assured them he was not, though that meant no big ransom would be forthcoming. They then forced him to write a letter to the rest of the Americans at the ranch but forbade him to mention Major Palmer's death. The ophthalmologist was also made to instruct the others to send out all their guns and ammunition for confiscation.

In an exchange of notes with the ranch, Dr Howard tried to convey by implication that Major Palmer was dead, though the bandit chief, Hai Feng, insisted that he declare the officer was alive and captured. Finally the bandits admitted Palmer's death but demanded the guns on pain of the doctor's safety. The Americans in the ranch agreed to pay what little money they had and hand over some antiquated ammunition. But even as the messenger was on his way, the bandits became nervous and took off.

After a rough and painful ride the band holed up in a house by the Sungari River. As they settled down in hiding, they interrogated Dr Howard about America and the rest of the world. 'They explained to me that the world was composed of five countries: China was the greatest, then came Russia, America, Great Britain, and Japan in the order of their importance. There used to be another country known as Germany, but China had a war with her a few years ago, and since then she had not been heard from.'

The bandits were most uneasy at having killed Major Palmer, since this would mean that a large number of soldiers would be sent out to destroy them, and the gang leader declared fatalistically (and prophetically): 'As bandits we are finished.'

Having lain down to sleep, the doctor noticed a sickly smell, and discovered that many of the recumbent bandits were smoking opium. His account of the process is worth reproducing:

> On each side of the room, stretched out on the smoking platforms, I saw a row of bandits. They had arranged themselves in pairs facing each other. Between each pair I saw a small, lighted peanut-oil lamp which was partly

covered with a paper shade. Each bandit held a long, slender wooden pipe, and was completely absorbed in drawing in fumes produced by holding the bowl of his pipe over the peanut-oil flame. The bowl of the pipe was a hollow drum, about an inch in height, with a small, round hole at the top. Over this hole was a cone-shaped mass of soft, dark brown substance about half an inch high, which sputtered in the heat of the flame. This brown substance, without a doubt, was crude opium. As the smoker inhaled, he manipulated the mass of opium with a probe to keep an air-hole open. Under the influence of the heat and the smoker's inhalations, the mass rapidly disappeared from the outer margin of the bowl. The smoker then removed the bowl from the stem of the pipe, and scraped the inside of the bowl with an instrument designed for this purpose. His manipulation brought forth a quantity of opium about one-half in amount as compared with the original mass. He molded this into a second cone with his fingers as one does putty. He then stuck the cone onto the bowl of his pipe over the hole in the same position that the original cone had been set before. With his fine probe he opened a small channel or air-hole from the apex of the cone down into the chamber of the bowl. This done, he replaced the bowl on the stem of the pipe and resumed smoking. This process was repeated several times until the opium finally disappeared.

The medical man was surprised at how fit and strong the opium-smoking bandits looked, by contrast with the stereotyped picture of the smoker as an emaciated, pathetic weakling. Over the coming weeks, he would come to understand the intimate relationship between the men's way of life and their smoking habit.

The bandits ate boiled sweetcorn and drank water; anything else was considered luxury. Through most of the night they kept up a din of shouting and abusing each other and cleaning their rifles, so that it was almost impossible to sleep. Silence at last descended as the opium-drugged brains of the outlaws drifted into sleep.

The next day, having apparently decided that Dr Howard was more trouble than he was worth, the bandits took him off on horseback while cheerfully explaining to him that he was to be shot. He then had to undergo a lugubrious process of self-auction, at which they first ordered him to obtain $50,000 from his friends, but as the negotiations proceeded finally settled for $10,000 and spared his life.

The bandit captain demanded a free medical examination and massage of an injured joint. Dr Howard found that the man had several bullet wounds which could have proved fatal in a person of less robust constitution, in addition to having contracted syphilis and trachoma of both eyes. Other bandits had ringworm, gonorrhoea, intestinal parasites, gastric complaints caused by excessive opium smoking, smallpox scars — but trachoma (a disease causing hard pustules on the inner surface of the eyelids) was the most prevalent ailment.

The bandits were so impressed by Dr Howard's good physique, medical science, and knowledge of the Chinese language that they sent a small delegation to him after nightfall, asking him to become their chieftain. He understandably prevaricated. The next day he was given fresh eggs to eat; he dressed the hand of a soldier who had shot himself while cleaning his gun and was rewarded with some half-cooked pig tripes which he could not bring himself to swallow.

The bandit lair was visited by an opium collector whose business was to extract tribute from the local farmers, and deliver the drug to the outlaws.

> His coming produced no little excitement for many of
> the bandits had consumed their own supply, and were
> borrowing from the band's opium treasurer, or from
> other bandits. I was beginning to learn that this band
> had a company organization, with its officers, its bank
> account, and its own system of records and bookkeep-
> ing. A few of the brigands did not use opium, so they
> either took their share, when opium was being divided

up among the members of the company and loaned it out to their opium-smoking comrades, or permitted the opium treasurer to keep it — accepting a credit on his books in ounces of opium or dollars.

There was a howl of dismay from the bandits when the opium collector disclosed that he had brought only about half the requisite amount — some 270 egg-sized lumps wrapped up in oiled paper for some 300 to 400 bandits. The collector explained that only three days before, soldiers had come to the growing-point ostensibly to destroy the poppies, but instead had settled for confiscation of half the crop.

In an abortive attempt to capture Dr Howard's friends at their ranch, the bandits instead fell upon some soldiers and there was a running fight. The more astonishing was it for the eye-doctor to see two of the soldiers visiting the bandits' nest shortly after, smoking opium and chatting amiably with them!

The band then upped sticks and moved on — doubtless feeling that the secrecy of their hideout was compromised — feeding off mouldy sweetcorn and battling the myriad biting insects that assailed them. The American's discomfort was not alleviated by the bandits presenting him with a young and strong but totally blind horse, which naturally kept slipping and throwing him, despite being pushed and pulled and beaten by the brigands riding to the front and rear.

The band stopped at a remote spot where there were some tiny grass huts for shelter.

> I beheld there a terrible sight. It was a human form — a man hideous from skin unwashed for years, it seemed. He was nearly naked; only a ragged cloth partly covered his loins. His ankles were bound together with a short chain which clanked as he hobbled on all fours. He held out his filthy, crusted hands to the little fire that still burned, and whined piteously as his half-closed eye looked hopefully around.

The bandits embarked on a longboat on the river and were joined by a famous chieftain who declared that Dr Howard must be ransomed for a sum of no less than $100,000. Their journey ended at a swampy place on the banks of a tributary of the Sungari, where the bandits had built a small fort with walls of sod. The next day they spotted swamp fires lit in the distance by soldiers trying to discover their location and smoke them out. While the leaders decided what to do, a bandit captain showed Dr Howard the trachoma in his eyes, which the physician proceeded to relieve with hot compresses, though there was no hope of a cure without modern drugs. Dr Howard promised to treat him properly if he would come to Peking when their ordeal was over. The bandit then agreed to let the American share his tiny tent with him, as sleeping on the boat was intolerably uncomfortable. The swamp fire lit by the soldiers nearly reached the 'fort', but the wind turned just in time and it swept off in another direction.

During the night Dr Howard heard a group of bandits reciting famous poems and the *Analects* of Confucius to each other, showing they were not entirely devoid of education but had been forced by the condition of their time into the wretched life of the bandit — for certainly no-one could call it fun to play Robin Hood in China.

The doctor noticed that though the bandits came to him for treatment of wounds and external ailments, internal troubles they invariably took to the practitioners of traditional Chinese medicine. Cauterization, pinching of the skin, acupuncture, or knotting thread through holes in the skin — the pain of the treatment was so severe that the patient often rejected further such torture and declared himself cured. When Dr Howard achieved better results with nothing more than applications of hot water, the traditional practitioners averred that his treatment made it uncomfortable for the 'devils' within and forced them out, thus curing the condition.

The most popular topic of conversation among the bandits was opium, for many of them had developed an addiction to it and were constantly discussing the price and location of future supplies, as Western soldiers might discuss liquor.

> Opium smoking seemed to fill their every need. It often took the place of food, sleep and recreation with them. In fact every necessity and all other luxuries were as nothing compared to the indulgence in this one vice. When they had plenty of crude opium, their happiness appeared to be complete. When they were without it, they were demons to live with. Undoubtedly the craving for this drug had driven many of them into the bandit business.

At long last a young officer of the Manchurian Army with two soldiers arrived at the encampment and calmly explained to the bandits that Dr Howard must be surrendered; he named each bandit and assigned a price on his head. The bandits were greatly alarmed at the threat to take hostages from their families in their home village, who were evidently known to the authorities, but instead of agreeing to release their American prisoner, they made quick preparations for departure. On reaching the Sungari River again, they saw to their dismay a gunboat and has tily made tracks back to escape its notice. With soldiers drawing ever nearer, the band made a desperate rush for safety. One of their Chinese hostages could not stand the pace, and this led to a shocking atrocity witnessed by Dr Howard.

The hostage was given a big pellet of opium to eat, but this did not sustain him for long. The chief bandit then ordered a grave dug; the trembling hostage was ordered to get into it, then thrown and kicked in when he refused. The bandit raised his axe and, as the shocked American looked away, brought it down on the hostage's skull ten times with horrifying sounds.

Ever more hotly pursued, the bandits took to the hills, terrified now of the approaching soldiers. Though they dodged hither and thither, there was a growing feeling of doom, so

that one of the chieftains asked Dr Howard to take with him
— should he escape or be rescued — a large package of raw
opium, for it would fetch a higher price in Peking than in
Manchuria and would enable the outlaw to emigrate to
America! The doctor declined.

The bandits occupied an abandoned cabin and set up a
crude shrine with an auspicious inscription, at which many
of them prayed for salvation. Then a messenger arrived from
the bandit-suppression troop, offering them amnesty and
positions in the official army if they would release their hostage. The bandits whooped with joy, for even the opium
smokers were promised enough of the drug to satisfy their
habit while in the army. But the negotiations fell through
and the bandits set off again on their weary chase through
the mountains.

Suddenly a man with a Mauser pistol dashed into a hut
where Dr Howard was forced to hide. 'We are soldiers, don't
fear!' he cried. With a crackle of gunfire the remaining bandits ran off with soldiers in pursuit. The American's ordeal
was over.

Some time later he received in Peking a letter from the
older bandit who had consented to share his tent with
him. The man wanted to know whether Dr Howard
could find him a job, as the gang had been dispersed. We
do not learn whether the eye-doctor complied with this
request.

Three facts of particular significance emerge from Dr
Howard's admirably clear and objective narrative. One is that
banditry in China held no glamour but was instead a hard,
probably short life, which no man in his senses would have
taken up if his existence as a civilian were not made intoler-
able by poverty and injustice.

Another point is that the bandits saw themselves as no
better or worse than the soldiery who hunted them down,
some of whom might well be bandits the next year. They
were rather poorly armed and terrified of modern methods
of warfare such as artillery, gunboats, and rapid-firing guns.

Almost the only consolation in their wretched lives was opium, and they would do anything to get it.

The third aspect of Chinese bandits which should be borne in mind is that there was obviously massive collusion between bandit gangs and the troops sent to suppress them, the regular soldiers helping themselves to other people's property almost as blithely as their supposed quarry did. But when there was political pressure from above, the officers and rank and file of the warlord armies were more than capable of tracking gangs down and killing or dispersing them, a fact clearly recognized by the often timorous outlaws.

6 The End of the Warlords

D R Sun Yatsen died in March 1925, but his dream of uniting China in a single republic did not die with him. General Chiang Kaishek was widely seen as the person best equipped to lead the military expedition needed to overthrow the northern warlords and introduce a republican form of government throughout China. A year later Chiang was formally appointed commander-in-chief, and in July 1926, the Northern Expedition set out to conquer its enemies — principally the forces of Wu Peifu, Zhang Zuolin, and Sun Chuanfang. Unknown quantities in the military equation were the Christian General Feng Yuxiang, the Shanxi *dujun* Yan Xishan, and the warlords of Sichuan, especially Liu Xiang and Yang Sen. Watching closely from the sidelines were the Russians, the Japanese, the British, and the Americans, the principal powers with interests in China.

Chiang knew he must eliminate Wu Peifu, who was the closest to south China, with his troops deployed in Hunan, Hubei, and Henan. Led by the courageous young officers who had been military cadets at the KMT military training school at Whampoa, near Canton, the Northern Expedition struck with lightning speed in Hunan and Hubei, and captured Wuhan in September. Chiang Kaishek, who saw Jiangxi province as the key to the war, took part of the army eastwards down the Yangtze River and after stiff fighting captured the provincial capital of Nanchang, proceeding to chase Sun Chuanfang out of Nanking. But as Chiang set about consolidating his position in east China, political divisions grew between him and the leftists in Wuhan, where the KMT government had been set up after the city's capture. Friction between the two wings of the expeditionary force grew until Chiang had Communists in Shanghai and other southern cities massacred without warning in April 1927. The Wuhan government 'dismissed' him, but it was a hollow challenge.

The convoluted role of the Chinese Communist Party in fighting the warlords came to an abrupt end. The decision, early in the life of the Party, to fight for the reunification of China under the banner of the KMT, at least in the first analysis, had led the Party to its own near destruction. The fact that this wrong path was the one advocated by Moscow, and carried out by the leadership of urban intellectuals, paved the way for the transformation of the Party into a peasant-based force.

Chiang and his supporters spent most of the next year consolidating their political position and rebuilding their forces for the second half of the Northern Expedition. In the spring of 1928, Feng Yuxiang's army led the attack on the positions of the eastern warlords Zhang Zongchang and Sun Chuanfang in Shandong. This, however, brought the KMT troops into conflict with Japan, which professed concern at the safety of its nationals still living in Shandong. That sparked the so-called Jinan Incident, in which Tokyo sent an expeditionary force to Shandong and in the ensuing fighting thousands of Chinese soldiers and civilians were killed and great damage was done to property. China and Japan were storing up grievances to fuel the war between them which was promising to break out on a large scale in the 1930s.

The only significant opposition to the Northern Expedition was now Marshal Zhang Zuolin, whose Manchurians were occupying Peking and the surrounding area. But Zhang saw the writing on the wall, and under diplomatic pressure from Japan he withdrew most of his army to his own northeastern base area. He was assassinated by the Japanese, who blew up his train on its way to Mukden (see Chapter 2).

The first expeditionary troops to enter Peking were those of Yan Xishan, from Shanxi, and Bai Chongxi from Guangxi. Peking surrendered peacefully and in due course the diplomatic corps extended its recognition to the KMT as the legitimate government of China. With the capture of Peking, Chiang Kaishek and the right-KMT had won the goals of the Northern Expedition.

At the end of the Northern Expedition in 1928 warlordism seemed to be over. This was the message that was reported to the spirit of Sun Yatsen, which lay in the Temple of the Azure Cloud in the Western Hills outside Peking. In a moving ceremony during which Chiang Kaishek actually threw himself on Sun's casket, Sun was told that his dream of reunifying China had been fulfilled.[1] This was not the case. Full control of the Chinese revolution still eluded the Kuomintang leaders. Of their main warlord enemies, one had already been assassinated — Zhang Zuolin. Two others, Zhang Zongchang and Sun Chuanfang, were still to meet a similar fate.

The ex-warlord Li Zongren had played an illustrious role in the Northern Expedition and was co-opted into the new government, though in positions of no great power (he lasted only until 1929). Feng Yuxiang abandoned his command and was never again a military force to be reckoned with. Zhang Zuolin's son took over the Manchurian army but professed loyalty to the Republic. Wu Peifu fled to Sichuan.

The main forces not yet under Chiang's control were the divided warlords of Sichuan, and Yan Xishan, who refused to give up the parts of Shanxi where his rule was effective. Yan fought the encroaching Japanese with tenacity in the 1930s, and after the defeat of Japan and the civil war of the late 1940s, he followed Chiang Kaishek to Taiwan where he died in 1960. The Sichuan warlords' troops were mostly absorbed into the KMT army when the government moved to Chongqing.

There was a question as to whether those who had simply changed their titles and their formal allegiance, but otherwise continued to behave as they had before, should still be called warlords or not. They probably should have been.

[1] Diana Lary, *Region and Nation, The Kwangsi Clique in Chinese Politics, 1925–1937*, Cambridge: Cambridge University Press, 1974, p. 116.

Even the KMT could be considered a warlord government, since it relied so heavily on military power and consistently put off moving towards the kind of popular, democratic government that Sun Yatsen had envisaged. But while it is true that Chiang Kaishek was always a military leader, and that he had little time for civilian processes, he did rule over a national government with specific political goals, one that differed in scale and in intent from the warlords.

Like violent children squabbling over the toys in a nursery, the warlords were quelled by the arrival of the grown-ups — the battle-hardened KMT, the Communists, and later the Japanese imperial army. The big issues of China's future were determined by these forces, not by the warlords, whose patriotism had been proved a sham masking their own vanity, greed, and frequent stupidity. Military men generally make poor administrators. In China the succession of military rulers, from Yuan Shikai on, impoverished the country and gave rise to four decades of war and civil war. The ancient, anti-military prejudices of the peasantry and the intelligentsia were once more confirmed by the savagery of history.

Glossary

Pinyin	Wade-Giles	Other
Anfu	An-fu	
Anguojun	An-kuo-chun	
Anhui	An-hui	Anhwei
Bai Chongxi	Pai Ch'ung-hsi	
Baoding	Pao-ting	
Beijing	Pei-ching	Peking
Beiyang	Pei-yang	
Bohai	Po-hai	
Cai E	Ts'ai O	
Cao Kun	Ts'ao K'un	
Chahar	Ch'a-har	
Changsha	Ch'ang-sha	
Chen Guangyuan	Ch'en Kuang-yuan	
Chen Yi	Ch'en Yi	
Chen Jiongming	Ch'en Chiung-ming	
Chengdu	Ch'eng-tu	
Chongqing	Ch'ung-ch'ing	Chungking
Cixi	Ts'u-hsi	Yehonala
Dalian	Ta-lien	Dairen, Dalny
Duan Chikui	Tuan Chih-k'ui	
Duan Qirui	Tuan Ch'i-jui	
dujun	tu-chun	
Feng Guochang	Feng Kuo-ch'ang	
Feng Yuxiang	Feng Yu-hsiang	
Fengtian	Feng-t'ien	

Fu Liangzuo	Fu Liang-tso	
Fujian	Fu-chien	Fukien
Gansu	Kan-su	
Guangdong	Kuang-tung	Kwangtung
Guangxi	Kuang-hsi	Kwangsi
Guangzhou	Kuang-chou	Canton
guanxi	kuan-hsi	
Guizhou	Kuei-chou	Kweichow
Guilin	Kuei-lin	Kweilin
Guo Songling	Kuo Sung-ling	
Guomindang	Kuo-min-tang	Kuomintang
Guominjun	Kuo-min-chun	
Han	Han	
Hankou	Han-k'ou	Hankow
Hangzhou	Hang-chou	Hangchow
Hebei	Ho-pei	Hopeh
Heilongjiang	Hei-lung-chiang	Heilungkiang
Henan	Ho-nan	Honan
Huang Shaoxiong	Huang Shao-hsiung	
Hubei	Hu-pei	Hupeh
Hunan	Hu-nan	
Jinan	Chi-nan	Tsinan
Jiangxi	Chiang-hsi	Kiangsi
Jiangsu	Chiang-su	Kiangsu
jiedusi	chieh-tu-ssu	
Jilin	Chi-lin	Kirin
Jiujiang	Chiu-chiang	Kiukiang
Kaifeng	K'ai-feng	
Kangxi	K'ang-hsi	
Li Chun	Li Ch'un	
Li Dazhao	Li Ta-chiao	
Li Zongren	Li Ts'ung-jen	

Li Yuanhong	Li Yuan-hung	
Liu Bang	Liu Pang	
Liu Xiang	Liu Hsiang	
Liaoning	Liao-ning	
Longtan	Lung-t'an	
Loyang	Lo-yang	
Lu Rongting	Lu Jung-t'ing	
Manzhouguo	Manchukuo	Manchuria/ Manzhouli
Mao Zedong	Mao Tse-tung	
Nanchang	Nan-ch'ang	
Nanjing	Nan-ching	Nanking
Ni Sichong	Ni Ssu-ch'ung	
Pukou	P'u-k'ou	
Puyi	P'u-i	
Qin	Ch'in	Tsin
Qing	Ching	
Qingdao	Ch'ing-tao	Tsingtao
Rehe	Je-ho	Jehol
Shaanxi	Shan-hsi	Shensi
Shandong	Shan-tung	Shantung
Shanhaiguan	Shan-hai-guan	
Shanghai	Shang-hai	
Shanxi	Shan-hsi	Shansi
Shenyang	Shen-yang	Mukden
Sichuan	Ssu-ch'uan	Szechwan
Sima Qian	Ssu-ma Ch'ien	
Song	Sung	
Suiyuan	Sui-yuan	
Sun Chuanfang	Sun Ch'uan-fang	
Sun Zi	Sun Tzu	

Sun Zhongshan	Sun Chung-shan	Sun Yatsen
Taierzhuang	Tai-er-chuang	
Taiping	T'ai-p'ing	
Tan Yankai	T'an Yen-k'ai	
Tang	T'ang	
taochi	t'ao-ch'ih	
Tianjin	T'ien-chin	Tientsin
Wang Jingwei	Wang Ching-wei	
Wang Ruxian	Wang Ju-hsien	
Wu Peifu	Wu P'ei-fu	
Wuchang	Wu-ch'ang	
Wuhan	Wu-han	
Xia Chao	Hsia Ch'ao	
Xian	Hsi-an	Sian
Xiang Yu	Hsiang Yu	
Xinjiang	Hsin-chiang	Sinkiang
xiucai	hsiu-ts'ai	
Xu Shichang	Hsu Shih-ch'ang	
Xu Xiangqian	Hsu Hsiang-chien	
Xuzhou	Hsu-chou	Hsuchow
Yan'an	Yen-an	Yenan
Yan Xishan	Yen Hsi-shan	
Yang Sen	Yang Sen	
Yangzi	Yang-tzu	Yangtze
Ye Ting	Yeh T'ing	
yuan	yuan	
Yuan Shikai	Yuan Shih-k'ai	
Yunnan	Yun-nan	
Zhang Guotao	Chang Kuo-t'ao	
Zhang Huaizhi	Chang Huai-chih	
Zhangjiakou	Chang-chia-k'ou	Kalgan
Zhang Jingyao	Chang Ching-yao	
Zhang Xueliang	Chang Hsueh-liang	

Zhang Xun	Chang Hsun
Zhang Zongchang	Chang Ts'ung-ch'ang
Zhang Zuolin	Chang Tso-lin
Zhili	Chih-li
Zhongnanhai	Chung-nan-hai
Zhuang	Chuang
zijue	tzu-chueh
Zunyi	Ts'un-i

Bibliography

Abend, Hallett, *My Life in China 1926–1941*, New York: Harcourt Brace, 1943.

Bland, J.O.P., *China, Japan and Korea*, London: Heinemann, 1921.

Brook, Timothy, *Quelling the People: The Military Suppression of the Democracy Movement*, Toronto: Lester Publishing Ltd, 1992.

Chang Chun-ku, *Wu Pei-fu chuan*, Taipei: Biographical Studies, 1980.

Chang Kuo-t'ao (Zhang Guotao), *The Rise of the Chinese Communist Party* (The Autobiography of Chang Kuo-t'ao), Lawrence: University Press of Kansas, Volume I, 1971; Volume II, 1972.

Ch'en, Jerome, *The Military–Gentry Alliance*, Hong Kong: Joint Publishing Co., 1979.

Ch'en, Jerome, *Yuan Shih-k'ai 1859–1916*, London: George Allen & Unwin, 1961.

Cheng Sih-gang, *Modern China*, Oxford: Clarendon Press, 1919.

Cherepanov, A.I., *Zapiski Voyennovo Sovietnika v Kitaye*, (Memoir of a Soviet Military Adviser in China), Moscow: Science Publishing House, 1976.

Ch'i, Hsi-sheng, *Warlord Politics in China 1916–1928*, Stanford: Stanford University Press, 1976.

Ch'ien, Youwen, *Feng Yu-hsiang Chuan*, Taipei: Biographical Press, 1982.

Cuenot, Rev. Joseph, *Au Pays des Pavillons Noires*, Hong Kong: Imprimerie de Nazareth, 1925.

Dingle, Edwin J., *China's Revolution, 1911–1912*, New York: McBride, Nat Co., 1912.

Drage, Charles, *Soldier of Fortune*, London: Heinemann, 1963.

Du Chunhe, Lin Pinsheng, and Qui Chuanzheng, eds.,

Beiyang junfa shiliao xuanji (Collected materials on the Northern Warlords), Chinese Social Sciences Publishing House.

Fairbank, John K., Reischauer, Edwin O. and Craig, Albert M. *East Asia: The Modern Transformation*, Tokyo: Charles E. Tuttle Co., 1965.

Feetham, Richard, *Report to the Shanghai Municipal Council*, Volume One, Shanghai: North China Daily News and Herald, 1931.

Forman, Harrison, *Report from Red China*, New York: Henry Holt, 1945.

Franck, Harry A., *Wandering in China*, London: and Fisher Unwin, 1924.

Franck, Harry A., *Roving Through Southern China*, London: The Century Co., 1925.

Frey, General H., *L'armée Chinoise*, Paris: Hachette, 1904.

Gillan, Donald G., *Warlord—Yen Hsi-shan in Shansi, 1911–1949*, Princeton: Princeton University Press, 1967.

Howard, Harvey J., *Ten Weeks with Chinese Bandits*, London: John Lane/The Bodley Head, 1926.

Hewlett, Sir Meyrick, *Forty Years in China*, London: Macmillan, 1943.

Hook, Brian, ed., *The Cambridge Encyclopaedia of China*, Cambridge: Cambridge University Press, 1982.

Hsu, Immanuel C.Y., *The Rise of Modern China*, New York: Oxford University Press, 1970.

Hu Boli, *Yuan Shikai cheng-di ji qi baiwang*, (Yuan Shikai's Self-Acclamation as Emperor, and his Defeat), Zhengzhou: Henan People's Publishing House, 1981.

Impey, Lawrence, *The Chinese Army as a Military Force*, Tientsin: Tientsin Press, 1926.

Jordan, Donald A., *The Northern Expedition: China's National Revolution of 1926–28*, Honolulu: University Press of Hawaii, 1976.

Kapp, Robert A., *Szechwan and the Chinese Republic: Provincial Militarism and Central Power, 1911–1938*, New Haven:

Yale University Press, 1973.

Koo, Madame Wellington (with Isabella Taves), *No Feast Lasts Forever*, New York: Quadrangle, 1975.

Kotenev, Anatol M., *The Chinese Soldier*, Shanghai: Kelly & Walsh, 1937.

Krarup-Nielsen, A., *The Dragon Awakes*, London: The Bodley Head Ltd., 1928.

Lary, Diana, *Region and Nation, The Kwangsi Clique in Chinese Politics, 1925–1937*, Cambridge: Cambridge University Press, 1974.

Lary, Diana, *Warlord Soldiers*, Cambridge, Cambridge University Press, 1985.

Liu F.F., *A Military History of Modern China*, Princeton: Princeton University Press, 1956.

McCormack, Gavan, *Chang Tso-lin in Northeast China, 1911–1928*, Stanford: Stanford University Press, 1977.

Martin, Bernd, *Die Deutsche Beratersschaft in China, 1927–1938*, Düsseldorf: Droste, 1981.

Mi Zanchen, *The Life of General Yang Hucheng*, Hong Kong: Joint Publishing Co., 1981.

Peck, Graham, *Through China's Wall*, Boston: Houghton Mifflin, 1941.

Pye, Lucian W., *Warlord Politics: Conflict and Coalition in the Modernization of Republican China*, New York: Praeger, 1971.

Rasmussen, A.H., *China Trader*, New York: Crowell, 1934.

Reinsch, Paul S., *An American Diplomat in China*, New York: Doubleday, 1922.

Seton, Grace Thompson, *Chinese Lanterns*, London: The Bodley Head, 1924.

Sheridan, James E., *Chinese Warlord: The Career of Feng Yu-hsiang*, Stanford: Stanford University Press, 1966.

Sheridan, James E., *China in Disintegration: The Republican Era in Chinese History 1912–1949*, London: Collier Macmillan, 1975.

Sichuansheng wenshi yanjinguan, *Sichuan junfa ziliao*, Chengdu: People's Publishing House, 1981.

Sladkovsky, M.I., ed., *Noveyshaya Istoriya Kitaya 1928–49* (Contemporary History of China), Moscow: Far Eastern Institute, 1984.

Sutton Donald, *Provincial Militarism and the Chinese Republic: The Yunnan Army, 1905–1925*, Ann Arbor: University of Michigan Press, 1980.

Tao Zhuyin, *Beiyang junfa tongzhi shiqi shihua* (Historical Talks on the Period of Rule of the Northern Warlords), Peking: Health, Reading and New Knowledge Three Unities Publishing House, 1958 (in 8 volumes).

Taylor, E., *The Struggle for North China*, New York: Institute of Pacific Relations, 1949.

Tuchman, Barbara W., *Stillwell and the American Experience in China, 1911–45*, New York: Macmillan, 1971.

Twitchett, Denis, and Fairbank, John K., (eds.), *The Cambridge History of China*, Vol. 12: *Republican China 1912–1949*, Part I, Cambridge: Cambridge University Press, 1983.

Weale, B.L. Putnam, *The Fight for the Republic in China*, London: Hurst & Blackett, 1918.

Whitson, William W. (with Chen-hsia Huang) *The Chinese High Command: A History of Communist Military Politics, 1927–72*, New York: Praeger, 1973.

Wilson, Dick, *When Tigers Fight: The Story of the Sino–Japanese War 1937–1945*, Penguin, 1983.

Wou, Odoric, *Militarism in Modern China: The Career of Wu P'ei-fu*, New York; Columbia University Press, 1978.

Yefimov, G., *Ocherki po Novoy is Noveyshey Istorii Kitaya* (Studies in Modern and Contemporary Chinese History), Moscow: State Publishing House for Political Literature, 1951.

Young, Ernest, *The Presidency of Yuan Shi-kai: Liberalism and Dictatorship in Early Republican China*, Ann Arbor: University of Michigan Press, 1977.

Yunnan junfashi yanjiuhui, *Xinan junfashi yanjiu congkan*, Kunming; Yunnan People's Publishing House, 1985.

Zhang Cheng, ed., *Zhang Zuolin*, Shenyang: Liaoning People's Publishing House, 1981.

Index